Josephine McC
Magical Knowledge
Book I
Foundations/
The Lone Practitioner

Mandrake

In this series
Magical Knowledge Book II - The Initiate
Magical Knowledge Book III - Adepts

Dedicated to
Lawrence Dunne, my father,
who opened Pandora's Box for me

Acknowledgements

Thanks to Ruth and Michael Collins (my neighbors and pseudo parents), and Toni Paris who bullied, cajoled and bribed me to get writing and quit stalling, to Mogg for being a great publisher, To Bob Gilbert for being, well, Bob Gilbert really, to Christin Cleaver, Anthony Thompson, Margie McArthur, John Plummer, Chris Giroux, Robert and Lorraine Henry for being such good magical friends, To Stuart Littlejohn for being the wonderful magical artist that he is, and a very special thanks to my sister Cecilia, who rescued me when I was drowning.

Contents

Foreword To
Magical Knowledge

I find it strange indeed, and oddly disquieting, to be writing a foreword for an author whose views — at least in her chosen field — are so decidedly at odds with my own, but there it is. How it came about that I should be doing this is an odd tale in itself. We met many years ago at Findhorn, that cosmopolitan haven of alternative living that epitomises New Age unreason. Within the context of a conference loosely dedicated to the Western Mystery Tradition, Josephine was performing traditional Indian dance, while I was lecturing and presenting a workshop on the nature, creation and working of initiatic ritual. An unlikely basis, perhaps, for a friendship, but what we shared in common, apart from acquaintances, was a rooted and vocal distaste for the whole false glamour of the New Age way of life.

Our paths crossed periodically in the years that followed even though our respective ways diverged. In practical terms hers broadened while mine narrowed. But although our attitudes and beliefs are far, far apart, our friendship and mutual respect remain unchanged. What Josephine believes and does is set out fully in this book, but before I speak of it and give it the praise that it deserves, I must say something of my own beliefs and set out my own spiritual path.

I am, and have always been, a practising Christian, but I do not believe that my faith makes me morally or spiritually perfect. Like all of humanity I am an imperfect being. I strive, not always successfully, to follow the moral code of the Christian faith, but I do not confine my practice of Christian morality to the material world alone. There are other, non-empirical, spiritual realms that I endeavour to explore and understand, and I do not believe that I am forbidden by my faith from doing so. What I am not is a magician.

There are ways of entering and exploring the spiritual world, and of encountering its inhabitants, that do not depend on the practice of magical ceremonies. These paths constitute the practical work of Christian esotericism, and those who engage with it ground their work in Divine Grace and perceive their chosen path as a way of return to God. For the magician, the centre of his or her working is the self, and the powers nascent within it or drawn down into it. Of course, this is a crude and far from adequate distinction between what I may term – again somewhat arbitrarily – the magical and the mystical paths, and I fully realise that there is much to be debated about the philosophical positions held by their respective followers.

What must be faced on both of these paths are the traps, pitfalls and dangers common to all exploration of the spiritual worlds. No one who enters those worlds can avoid these unwelcome encounters. I know from experience that they are all too real, but there are ways of overcoming them appropriate to one's chosen path. This is not, however, the place to discuss my personal approach, for this is not my book. Indeed, I have never written for the public on the practicalities of ceremonial esoteric work, whether institutional or personal, for I look upon my work as private. This is not so much a matter of reticence or a desire for exaggerated secrecy as the simple fact that I am primarily an historian who has chosen to write about magical, masonic and esoteric Orders – especially those of the last two hundred years. Thus, what I know of the Hermetic Order of the Golden Dawn is derived substantially from manuscript records and the reminiscences of surviving members of its early offshoots. That what I have written has been of benefit to various modern Orders, some of which have rewarded me with unasked for honorary membership, is an accident of history.

Here I should insert a caveat on 'secret' Orders, one that you will not find repeated in this book. Long ago I entered Freemasonry, of the established, 'regular' variety, and gradually branched out into some of its many exotic offshoots. They were fascinating and membership of them was, to a degree, enjoyable. But of esoteric or spiritual content they were effectively empty. It is true that many real adepts of the past, whether magicians such as Dion Fortune or mystics such as A.E. Waite, have looked upon Freemasonry as a solid foundation on which to build a sound ceremonial structure. Today, alas, it would result only in a house built upon sand. Whatever spiritual force or esoteric power there may have been is now wanting. To the grandees of masonic Grand Lodges the very words 'esoteric' and 'spiritual' are anathema and while the original ethos of the Order – to mould upright, moral and honourable men – is admirable, it has degenerated into an empty vessel offering only social functions and a meaningless hierarchical ladder. The masonic initiate is 'taught to be cautious', and I would urge any who may look upon Freemasonry as a way of entry into truly esoteric Orders to exercise due caution and not to take up this ancient but empty shell.

Equal caution should, of course, also be applied to every esoteric or magical Order that may appear on your horizon. Magic is currently very much in fashion and there are many who desperately seek for instruction in its working and who clamour for initiation into one or another magical Order, but I am not the person to guide them. It is not my way and most magical Orders I would shun like the plague, but while I might disapprove of a chosen path, I would never interfere with your right to follow it. Even so, I would be shirking my duty if I did not offer advice and informed opinion, all of which each and every one of you may accept or reject as you choose.

If you set out on the magical path you will almost certainly ignore my words and turn instead to an avowed and experienced magician: just such a one as Josephine McCarthy. Here you have a book that will help you and an author whose views you can respect. More than this, you may safely trust her practical guidance, which is drawn from a long and varied experience of working alone and with others. She is a gifted teacher, perceptive and critical, and well able to distinguish the hallmarks of a true adept from the counterfeit glamour of the moral pygmies who strut and pose as self-proclaimed Magi. Perhaps more important, she is also human. Thus, much as I admire her, I disagree profoundly with her interpretation and understanding of Christianity and its history, which she has an unfortunate tendency to misconstrue and so to misrepresent. It is done honestly enough, but I would be denying my faith if I did not emphasise that Christianity, even in the established Churches, is not all one-sided. Mercy and justice *are* properly tempered, religion is not necessarily divorced from spirituality, and the Church is not solely about power – it is also about enabling communities of believers to work effectively together. The horrors inflicted in the name of Christianity – and of *all* religions, for that matter – are the work of human beings who distort the essence of the very faith they profess to hold. It is precisely because of human wickedness, which no moral relativism can deny, that we need to engage with our chosen spiritual path for the benefit of humanity.

So, to the book. The aim of *Magical Knowledge* is to introduce the novice to the essence of magic, its underlying theory no less than its practical application, and to guide him or her through the minefield of dangers and distractions – not least the Goblin Market of shrilly competing peddlers of occult wares – to the attainment of magical wisdom. As a guide to the lone practitioner of magic it is comprehensive, sensible and straightforward. More than this, it is also both timely and necessary, for the proliferation of internet sites offering instant magical competence – at a price – present a threat not only to the pockets of seekers but also to their psycho-spiritual integrity.

What, then, does Josephine McCarthy present? Beginning with a stage by stage introduction to what magic is and how the would-be magician should approach it – why, for example, does the seeker want to be a magician? – she emphasises the need for personal responsibility, the matter of magical ethics, the setting of boundaries in relation to the power of magic, and the problems and dangers of the abuse of that power. Then there is the question of our interaction with entities of other realms, both human and non-human, and how, if at all, it is to be conducted. But before all of this is approached one crucial issue is addressed: 'The Pitfalls and Traps of Magic'. It is a chapter that can save the unwary explorer of occultism, whether magician, mystic or more general esotericist, from loss and damage of many kinds.

In trenchant and often picturesque language Josephine excoriates the manipulators, the showmen and the frauds of the magical world. She derides what she calls 'Candy Shop Magic' – the amassing of elaborate and *outré* regalia, implements and the detritus of commercial occultism for their own sake; she warns against grandiose but puerile Orders that publicly advertise themselves as being the 'true' remnant or descendant of great Orders of the past; and she rightly dismisses the notion of do-it-yourself initiation. With all of this I fully agree.

Just as one cannot be one's own initiator, so there can be no internet initiation or digital development in the esoteric field. Self-styled adepts and gurus are invariably worthless and inevitably cause untold psycho-spiritual damage to the neophyte. Only if an esoteric Order is entered in due form and with full knowledge of its pedigree, what to expect of it, and what must be brought into it, can the initiate feel secure that he or she is in a safe and informed esoteric environment. Only under these conditions can we learn from teachers whom we have come to respect. Such learning does not come from mail order manuals.

It can, of course, also come from personal effort and experience when one works alone – provided there is a reliable and supportive guide at hand. And this is where *Magical Knowledge* excels. The second part of the book is given over to the work of the lone practitioner, who is guided through the methodology of lone working, introduced to the necessary elements of personal ceremonial working, shown in great detail and depth what is required for two major aspects of such work – Visionary Magic and Ritual Magic – and provided with solid instruction in the use and understanding of the Tarot.

Thus far and no farther. But what more can the novice need? Whether one engages with magic or puts it at arm's length there is no question but that the magical path is a hard road that requires dedication, discrimination and a solid dose of common sense. The path that Josephine maps out is not the road for me, but if you are determined to follow the magical path, and if you employ these three qualities, you will be hard pressed indeed to find a better guide.

R.A. Gilbert, Tickenham, August 2011

"No enunciation of the Truth will ever be complete, no method of training will ever be suitable for all temperaments, no one can do more than mark out the little plot of infinity which he intends to cultivate, and thrust in the spade, trusting that the soil may eventually be fruitful and free from weeds so far as the bounds he has set himself extend..."
— Dion Fortune

Introduction

Magical training these days is available in a wide variety of forms be they local classes, internet study groups or expensive weekend intensives. The cost also varies from small donations to literally thousands of pounds/dollars and the old wisdom 'a fool and his money is easily parted' really becomes obvious. So how should someone, who seeks magic from the bottom of their hearts, navigate their way through this minefield of commercialism, New Age bunkum and con artist gurus? Well, basically use your common sense and don't let the powerful yearning within you cause your bullshit meter to turn off.

These days you can learn alone or in a group, or a combination of both but there is one really really important point that needs to be absorbed and understood; magic is not about paths, rules and dogma. Magic is the understanding of how the world works from an inner point of view; it is a true hybrid between spirituality and science. Magic is about the Divine Power that hangs the universe together- magic or spirituality speaks to that power and science quantifies that power. Once that is understood, then it truly becomes apparent to the seeker when a supposed school of magical thought is actually a school of magical dogma that seeks to mould individuals to its agenda. A true magical school will teach techniques and methods that are related to the culture from which the community springs. A true magical school will not tell its students that it is the only way, or that walking away from that path will bring dire consequences, or that it is the holder of various secret magical revelations. All such claims should set off the bullshit alarm and the hand of reason should swing from the sky and slap you joyously around the back of your head.

Many different schools will give you many different things and my advice is to start at the beginning with a well-known and respected group or school to learn the very basics, or at least some good basic books. That gives you a structure to work from and will give you an idea of what is happening in the universe. Just be aware that many schools these days offer 'training to the highest levels of magic' and that with them you can become an adept in 3 years. If you see such claims, walk away quickly because they are full of shit. In my opinion (which is not humble), schools are useful only for the basic foundation of magic. After that, an individualist's path with inner guidance and outer helpful people will be far more useful for magical training. The other dynamic with that approach is that when you call out to the inner worlds for a teacher, one will cross your path when it is time to really get your ass in gear and learn the serious stuff - you are never really alone with magic.

This book is divided into two parts. The first half of the book is about the general magical pitfalls, mess ups, explanations about how things work and why, how the inner worlds work and what they are, and a brief outline of the beings you can expect to meet in the inner worlds. Throughout the book you will find advice regarding 'rules', boundaries and how things work. Because this book is aimed at people in the early stages of serious magical study, those rules are there to provide a ring fence around the practitioner for their own safety. There will come a time when you decide that a rule no longer applies and that is valid providing that you have accomplished the task within the rule structure so that you fully understand the power dynamics; that ensures that you stay alive and do not damage yourself of those around you.

The second half of the book is about how to teach yourself how to acquire certain magical techniques, explanations of how to make things work and advice about the various areas of magical study. Basic but potentially powerful techniques are combined with some exercises to give the reader a path of work to begin with. Working with these techniques will very likely put you on a path to finding a decent magical teacher who will guide you through the next magical phase of your life.

Magic has been my life from being very young, and I can say that it has enriched my life to a level that is almost indescribable; I cannot imagine life without magic. The path was and still is tough, mainly walked alone with the odd eccentric teacher thrown in my path when I needed them, and it has challenged my courage, strength and values to levels that almost broke me at times. I think it has made me a better person and it most certainly made me feel whole: it is like coming home. Magic is my life.

1

The World of Magic and Magical Training

Things to Consider

The first exposure of a person to magic these days is usually through a book or a film and then a desire for something which we all know instinctively, deep inside us, is powerful, natural and true. Gone are the days when the lords of the manor secretly held all the mysteries of ritual magic and the villagers held the magical secrets of the land powers. In the last hundred years magic has gone public, it has appeared in college courses, night classes, 'how to' books, films, t-shirts, the list is as endless as a compulsive shopper's wish list. And therein lies the secret: magic is power, true magic, real magic. It is powerful, intense and dangerous. It is beautiful, inspiring and it brings us closer to ourselves.

Although the average person in the street is exposed only to the cotton candy variety of magic, their instincts, deep instincts, tell them to fear or desire it. Such fear is of course partly grounded in the fears fed to us as children, and the propaganda fed to us by the Church. Yes magic is dangerous in its full potential, yes it can do the soul damage if misused, and yes there are unethical people out there who use it. But the same could be said of a car. And if a child gets into a car, the worst thing that could happen is they take the handbrake off and roll. A car needs keys, and it needs skills to drive it. Once those skills are honed to a fine art, they can be used for great good or great bad. They can also be used simply to do a necessary job.

The majority of people who are first drawn to magic fall into either the witchcraft collection of paths (Wicca, Trad Craft, etc), or the ritualist collection (Golden Dawn, OTO etc). On line courses and book series proliferate and eventually people find their way to a local group or a more solid course of study. From that point they usually join a coven or a lodge.

The commercialisation of magic has brought about a massive change in how magic is approached, and why. It has been watered down to make it more palatable, it has been discussed in psychological terms to make it more believable and it has been presented to make it the panacea for all ills. The dogmas have been reinforced, the snake oil pocketed and the profits made. Magic is so much more than that. Magic is the power that flows from un-being into being. Magic is the space between objects, planets and cells. Magic is the logic of the universe.

Many of the systems of magic that have developed over the millennia were originally designed in relation to the land on which the magician lived and what culture he or she was immersed in. The cultural relationship with divinity was the vessel that held the magical system, and religion/magic were one and the same thing. The separation between deity and magic is a relatively recent thing and has been a slow but sustained split in the various schools of magic.

This movement away from the central culture and religious expression of the people slowly developed magic as a hidden power that was potentially evil, and something that only 'bad' people do. This attitude developed steadily in the monotheistic religions, so we go from Moses, Aaron and Miriam, the mythical three magicians who mediated magical power in a battle for their people, through to Jesus who used magic, along with other religious revolutionaries of that time (Simon Magus is one good example), to the purging of all magical/mystical texts and people during the expulsion of the heretics in both Judaism and early Christianity. It was at this point that magic and religion in the Western world parted ways.

Because of this expulsion of heresies, magic became furtive and mobile. It was passed quietly on from generation to generation by people who moved around from one land to another. So for example, Jewish people traveling around Europe took their own brand of magic with them and began practicing and teaching it upon the new land where they lived. This had a great effect upon the people whom they interacted with and magical wisdoms were passed back and forth and sometimes melded together. One very good example of this is Italy in the 15th century when Sephardic Jews were cast out of Spain and ended up in Italy via Libya. The interaction between Libyan Berbers, Spanish Catholics and the Jewish Kabbalists is very apparent in the magic of that time which gave birth to the Keys of Solomon.

The magic of those Kabbalists from the 15th century still has a great deal of influence on the magic of today: the Keys of Solomon and related texts are considered the cornerstone of certain types of magic. Egyptian writings relating to magic/religion that were unearthed in the 1800s by esoteric archaeologists and Romantics also play a heavy part in modern magic. Today, people follow those paths of magic because they are known and they work.

Magic is an expression of power and of how that power relates to you, your environment and the ancestors. Magic is the interface of the land and divinity; it is the power of the elements around you, the power of the Sun and Moon, the air that you breathe and the language of the unseen beings, both benign and malicious that are living alongside you. With all that in mind, how valid is it to then try and interface with this power by using a foreign language, foreign deities, and directional powers that have no relevance to the actual land upon which you live? The systems will work, and sometimes very powerfully, but how does it affect the land and ourselves? I am not saying that to use these systems is wrong; I use them in various ways myself. But I think it is important to be very mindful of where and what you are, and to build upon that foundation.

So if you were beginning to practice magic in steps, beginning with opening and closing the directions, instead of copying something from another land, stop and look at what is around you. Where is the water in relation to you, where are the plains or grasslands, where is the Sun, where are the burials, where are the mountains. Look at what ancient things are around you, what ancestral contacts are there. Do you have cemeteries, cairns, ancient remains, burials, castles etc. Look at maps to see what natural springs are around you, are there any caves etc. If you are in a city that is modern and vast, like an American city, look into its history to see what is there. It is not easy to find the ancient stories of a land but if you dig with intent to work with it, powers will begin to awaken to help you.

When I lived in Tennessee, I had a hell of a job trying to find local information but after digging relentlessly, I did come across some very interesting details that really slotted together very well and gave me a template to work from upon that land. Another very important point to consider is manners. If you work to find what is actually on the land, and who was there before you, how they did things, what were their legends etc, you will find that quite powerful forces begin to swirl around you in response. You will be led to places to experience things and the natural powers of magic within the land will open up to you. It is important that if these land powers awaken to you, that you are acutely aware of the manner of your communication towards them and that you are always respectful (so that they do not eat you).

Magical Systems, Old and New

One of the major problems that has repeated over and over within magical circles is the quick disintegration of a true magical system to either a commercial New Age venture, or the older story which is an infighting, agenda driven lodge. The first happens when the power input is imbalanced and the second usually happens either for the same reason or because the person who was holding it together died. Both pictures (and these are just two examples of what can go wrong, there are many more) display an inherent imbalance in the foundation of the system. Why the inherent imbalance? Because the foundations are built on shaky ground.

A great many magical systems work from the ground up, Kabbalah for example, trains the neophyte to slowly climb the Tree of Life through study, ritual and meditation. This works from the stance of the human body, which is a finite physical container for the soul, reaching up towards divinity. This creates a drag upon the body and is also like swimming up stream. When you work from the ground up, you are working within the burden of manifestation, and you have to carry that manifestation as a spirit form as you attempt to journey back to the threshold of divinity (the edge of the Abyss or Daarth).

The spirit naturally travels down the Tree on its journey into and through life. If you repeat this journey in a conscious way, you are more able to interact magically with the process, the beings involved and the powers as you pass from un-being into being. Dion Fortune was a great advocate of this method and from my own personal magical experience, I would say it is a far more powerful method and for me unlocked a great many of the magical secrets hidden within.

And yet, going from Malkuth upwards is the 'official' way to work the Tree. I am not saying that it does not work to study going up the Tree, but I am saying that it does fly against the natural flow of the Tree (which is not actually a tree or anything even remotely to do with trees). The other problem I see in Kabbalah training is that it encourages intense mental study which creates a trap whereby the mind is constantly swirling around concepts that only the spirit can truly open.

The second aspect of a shaky foundation is the magical container, i.e. the philosophies, myths and rituals that the system sits upon. Most Western magic comes from the line of systems that were developed out of mystical Christianity and Judaism, with some Greek, Roman and Egyptian threads thrown in for good measure. If you look into the deeper historic and magical aspects of all of these threads, the first thing that becomes apparent is the lack of proper polarity i.e. exclusion of women in their full power and the heavy reliance upon sovereignty power, which is essentially a power grab. So you have magical systems developing through a male line that is connected to religious and mythical patterns of power grabbing. Both patriarchy and matriarchy are imbalanced expressions of power and can both express imbalances through their actions, something that we have witnessed repeatedly throughout history.

The other problem with the basing of magic upon these mythical and religious foundations is that by the time the classical era came along, i.e. Greek/Roman era, these ancient patterns were already corrupt and degenerate. By the time the medieval era came along, it was truly stinking. Magic deals directly with power and with beings. When you look into Judaic and Egyptian history, you have to go back a pretty long way to find the time when there was a less dogmatic and manipulative relationship to power and beings. It is a pattern that repeats over and over in the Mediterranean and Near East cultures from about 500BC onwards (much earlier in some cases). These cultures and the degenerated myths are what our current magical systems are based upon. They are then imposed over a land that has no real connection to them.

So how does a neophyte or new initiate navigate such a vessel and do they actually need to? A system by which a person can learn about power structure is vitally important, just as religion is an important teacher for a person to learn about devotion. If they are approached with the pre warning about the pros and cons, the cracked vessel, then much learning can be brought out of working within such a container. The important step is to realize when it has given all that it can give and it is time for the initiate to step away and move on. There are also a great many lessons that can be learned from working with an unbalanced system, and learning first hand why it is imbalanced. Most people have a complex bag of learning needs when they first approach magic and the imbalanced paths can place those learning needs right in the face of the initiate if they choose to look. It's all about evolution.

That is not to say that we should stick with imbalanced paths because we can learn from them, any more than we should take heavy drugs to learn why not to take them. Some people need that 'in your face learning'; others have different burdens of learning that they need to shoulder. The adepts have a chance, if they take it, to strike out and wipe the slate clean by working on structural methods of learning magic that do not rely on these imbalanced paths. It is very hard work but does provide a healthier ladder for the initiate to climb, and it is a form of magical service to the next generation. For the neophyte or new initiate, the onus is to look beyond glamour and comfort zones, to find a system that is clean and as balanced as possible. Most of the magical systems of old present a wonderful glamour that attracts seekers like a golden Grail. It is up to the seeker to look beyond, and to question what it is they are actually looking for. If it is pure glamour, then such magical systems will suffice. If it is true magical learning a beginner seeks, then the search will become much harder and will have less outer gratification.

But with the quickly changing world in which we live, and with its more flexible way of being, there are many magical adepts from a variety of systems who are throwing the old order to the winds and trying to experiment, research and build more relevant and efficient working practices. The previous generations who attempted such vessel building often reverted to drawing upon history, myths, philosophies and more recently psychology in an attempt to forge a new path. I feel the problem with such an approach is that by reaching through texts/histories, we are already back to the issue of shaky foundations. This is reaching up the Tree from the ground, trying to swim against the tide. The answer, I feel, is to reach into the inner worlds, into the land and to access the deeper inner soul of ourselves, which is to go from the inner worlds, from the soul 'out of time' to get a deeper inner perspective of how the power flows into our world. That way, the adept can see at what point in the process the power begins to distort (so from a Kabbalistic point of view for example, at what section of the Tree does the power begin to fragment) and begin to work on a vessel that plugs that distortion, or dispenses with it entirely.

By working on the construction of a magical system before the powers manifest physically, the outer expression of that power finds its own natural form that is more in harmony with who we are and where we live.

Duality and ethics in magic

The major issue that people hit when they begin serious magical study is the issue of light/dark, good/bad, right/left hand path (a dyslexic's nightmare). Such separation of the two streams of power is inherently unhealthy and immediately creates an antagonism of power (although that antagonism can be seen as a power source by some magical paths). Either path studied to any depth will create an imbalance within which the natural flow of power will try to re harmonize itself. When this rebalancing manifests itself without the conscious actions or intentions of the magician, it can have a destabilizing effect and will play out in a number of different ways either through the life path of the practitioner or through their bodies as mental or physical imbalances. If a practitioner consciously engages the opposing flow of power through action and intent, it can have a more productive and educational effect.

Another way of avoiding imbalances is to completely sidestep the polarization and approach the light and dark equally, or to walk a path that works with beings unconditionally. The same method is also employed in the interaction of beings in the inner and outer worlds. Instead of viewing a being as inherently 'good' or 'bad', the practitioner works with each being without judgement and understands that every being has its role in the picture of existence. Just because a being or a being's expression of power is bad for humanity, does not make it bad, it is all relative. In practice this means working in all worlds with all beings in an appropriate way and simply understanding how they affect us, and how we affect them. Through that understanding you may choose to not work with certain beings because of how they affect us. That is not the same as the practice of subduing, pinning or binding a being just for being itself because it is considered 'dark'.

If a being of great power is causing chaos, the first question to ask would be why? If it is simply doing its own thing in the greater pattern, then it should not be interfered with just because we do not like it. If it is out of place because some human ritual action drew it in, then it should be quietly put back where it belongs (parasites for example). If it has been bound ritually into service by a human action and is causing chaos then it must be unbound and put back where it came from. If it has been released from a natural process of binding by ritual magic, then it needs to be put back into its binding. It's like returning things to factory settings.

Some beings, particularly strong ancient powers, are bound naturally by the evolution of species and the planet. To release them for conditional reasons is highly dangerous as they do not operate on our 'frequency' and can cause untold damage. This can manifest as a practitioner summoning and releasing ancient powers from the depths of the Abyss. It is all very 'glam' but creates a hell of a mess. And this is one of the approaches that has created such imbalance in our world; we cannot stop meddling to suit ourselves. Practitioners follow a path of light and dark, and from there, summon or, banish or bind beings that fit with their agenda. This is reflected in the Tibetan Buddhist practice of teaching respect for all beings, but then binding powerful beings into conditional service. Not healthy at all. It is much healthier, but harder, to meet and work with such beings on an equal footing, unconditionally, powerfully, and with respect.

In practical modern terms, the magical practitioner would learn about all the various orders of beings, meet them on their own turf (i.e. the Abyss) and learn the dangers of certain types of beings. From there, a wider understanding of how power and consciousness can develop, leading to healthier and more respectful practices.

Approach to training: selfish versus non selfish

Magic is simply the manipulation of power to illicit a change. The *elicit* change can be conscious, conditional, unconditional or unconscious. Magic moves power from A to B, it awakens powers and forces, or it sends them into hibernation. It evokes emotional responses, affects the human body, changes the flow of fate, brings things into being and sends them into un-being. It can build structures in other worlds and it can be used to interface with beings from other realms.

So immediately you can see how easily magic can be misused if someone with no ethics, loads of patience and natural talent decides to walk down that path.

There are two ways to approach magic; the intelligent way and the stupid way. To approach it the stupid way, the neophyte uses magic to obtain that which his personality is too weak to achieve alone without effort. As the neophyte progresses, the temptation and then justification to use magic to achieve whatever is needed becomes greater and more normalized. So if the magician is slighted, hurt or otherwise upset, then they will revert to aggressive magic to attack and punish. They will use magic to protect their physical territory from physical things i.e. put magic on something so it will not be stolen. Magic is used to draw in a lover, money, fame, and to settle disputes: the list is as endless as man's stupidity.

If this path is taken, there is no fatherly God sitting on a cloud wagging a parental finger. Life is not quite so easy. Magic is used for inner issues, not outer ones. What happens with such an approach to magical work is that the personality gradually gets weaker and the spirit gets flabbier. We learn, strengthen and mature from the physical knocks, hardships and disappointments that life puts in our path. Using magic to shortcut those lessons leaves a person emotionally, spiritually and magically illiterate. The personality that approaches magic to handle issues and problems is the same as the personality of a longterm drug user: their emotional age becomes stuck at the age when they started 'using'. They do not develop an 'inner skin' which is something that life knocks can give us, therefore they become vulnerable to inner parasites that feed off emotive, magical and sexual exchanges, and they then use that energy to cross dress in an effort to convince the practitioner that it is a magical contact/deity.

The combination of a retarded emotive age and inner parasites results in a very unhealthy and unhappy individual who 'bottoms out' in their magical power. It levels off at a dead end and they get stuck. It is nature's way of saving humanity from its own idiots. If they are naturally talented at magic, it can result in mental illness.

A more intelligent way is to approach magic like learning a craft that has an ancient heritage, and a lot of responsibility attached to it. If it is approached with a sense of respect and service, of wanting to be useful, then although such a path is not as materially rewarding, it is a very powerful path. A respect for the divinity within all things, a respect for the beings of all the different realms without judgement or prejudice, and a respect and willingness to protect/serve the world of nature around us are all foundations of approach which put the neophyte on a path of magical priesthood. It then links him to those who have walked the same path of service for millennia. It is not a fluffy bunny path by any means - the practitioner often serves deep and high in the Abyss, facing great danger. Such a path brings with it difficulties and challenges but it also brings with it great learning, power and maturity. The magician must be able to cross all realms, commune with all types of beings and be able to fight their corner in deep magical combat when needed. All of which needs to be done without any emotion.

So why do we do magic?

Humanity has an ability that many other beings, both physical and not physical do not have: we can move power and consciousness from A to B. We can initiate action, pressing the red button so to speak, which many other beings cannot do. Every being has its inner action and when all the beings and actions are put together you have an orchestra. Our part is to start the ball rolling and move power around. Magic forms a threshold and filter for power, it shapes it, patterns it, gives it form and brings it out into our world. It alters the flow of inner power and by ritual we can effect change in that power, give it boundaries and use it to a specific end.

With that in mind, the magician can use that ability to serve himself, or to serve the land, culture, community or divinity. It will work regardless of the intention but the long-term outcomes both for the individual and the land upon which they reside will be different. Often the magician will change intent over the years as the personality matures. Sometimes, of course, that doesn't happen and the magician stays on their original path of intent, be it good, bad or indifferent. If the magician develops along a path of unconditional magic, then their magical actions join the 'orchestra of power' and the intention is simply one of serving where it is needed and doing the work that is presented to them. Often (but not always) the result or conclusion of the work is unseen by the magician, and they just play their part.

Personal development

There is a stream of people who are drawn to magic because religion has failed them in some way and yet they are deeply aware that there is more to the world than Kentucky Fried Chicken. Often people have mystical, magical or power/sight experiences that show them, at a deep personal level, that there are streams of power that are not apparent and they begin to explore those streams.

In general, the Western culture in which we live is underpinned by a sense of powerlessness: the government runs our lives, the organized religions that control our access to divinity, and social constraints discourage use and expression of power. When a person chooses not to play a part in that circus they look elsewhere. Some people begin that path in search of their own power, some begin in search of knowledge and some approach that path from a sense of deep instinct.

The beginning of the path in magic is very much about personal development, be it spiritual, intellectual or self-determination. This is the first rung of the ladder and has many dead ends woven into it at a deep magical level regardless of the type of magic it is. These dead ends are designed to trap and teach them a lesson that is needful for their development. Some stay in those traps indefinitely (the inner weeding process) and some eventually get the message at a deep level and haul themselves up onto the next rung of the ladder. The 'dead ends' on the first rung of magic are often related to our relationship to power, glamour and ego. We all go through it in one form or another and most climb out of it with a very red face, ready to move on, lesson well learned. There is nothing wrong in making mistakes and doing silly things, it is all part of the learning process. The first rung teaches us about ourselves, our weaknesses and strengths, our true desires and fears, and the real extent of our ability to be honest with ourselves. Remember the words over the door to the temple: *Man, know thyself.* The threshold of the temple must be crossed with the intention to be willing to look in the mirror with an open mind and see what is really there.

If we approach the 'outer mysteries', which is the first rung of the ladder, with that openness we begin the focused evolution of the soul, which takes up the rest of our lives. Because the outer court of magic, or the outer/lesser mysteries contain methods of divination, methods of basic ritual, using magical tools, and the study of magical history, there are many who approach the first ladder and get stuck in these outer court skills. They can pull a few 'tricks', impress people with their titles, dress in cool clothes and have strange symbols around their necks: it is a power dead end for the ego. Some get stuck there for a time and climb out, and some stay there indefinitely.

When the initiate climbs out of that dead end, they look back and see the power traps, the allurement of the ego and they then have to face their weaknesses. That is a major step forward. Higher octaves of the same experience revisit the neophyte in a variety of ways until all the layers are peeled away. There is nothing wrong with ego, indeed it is something that is needful in our society and for ourselves: it is a natural and healthy part of our psychological make up. It is a problem when it becomes the 'truth' to us and we are unaware of it. The first layers of training expose the weakness and then the strengths of our egos. It takes fragmented egos and solidifies them, making a person confident with awareness from within, as opposed to trying to obtain confidence and power through outside actions.

When that rung of the ladder is finished, the new initiate climbs onto the next rung which is a higher octave of the first. The magical work becomes more about the group, or the community, or the lodge. The same traps are present, just in a more subtle dressing. The magical work becomes more focused through ritual and vision, through the use of the elements/tools, and the introduction to beings. This brings with it, particularly for the naturally inclined magician, the ability to move power around, contact inner beings and affect the world around them in small ways. They learn how to manipulate power and the very shiny dead end appears. Some magicians, at this phase, become very enamoured of their own ability and sense of importance. It is the all singing all dancing messiah trap. Their ability to impress people is strong and they are held in awe by people who are not of their level of knowledge. Some climb out of this dead end, again red faced and a little wiser. Some do not and become New Age pop star/goth/ guru/Merlin flavored magicians who effectively feed off the surrounding neophyte's energy.

The initiates who do not get stuck in this trap, or who climb out of it, learn how to use their ability and technique for the good of their community, land, lodge or group. At this phase, initiates are also sometimes given the responsibility to teach early neophytes which in itself is a major learning tool for the initiate. It is only when we have to teach something to another person that we really begin to see the mechanics of power, technique and method. If the initiate is not part of a magical order or group, i.e. a lone practitioner, the same power dynamics occur as it is part and parcel of the way inner power flows. Things are put in your path and you either learn from them or you don't. If you learn, more powerful things are put in your path and you step forward to the next training session. This rung is the usual one where initiates decide to leave the group or stream and go it alone. It is a harder path, but can for some be a much more powerful one.

The next and more powerful rung is the one of service to the long term planetary powers and to divinity. This is the level where magic and spirituality truly comes together and the adept becomes a true priest of universal power (not deity). The service is rarely conducted within a lodge or group, but becomes either a very lonely path or one whereby others of similar level are brought together from different streams to do a 'job', which can often span a whole lifetime. It fully dispenses with the dead end of egos because the simple nature of the work often demands a silence in the outside world. This is not an oath form of secrecy; rather it is a knowing that there is nothing to be gained and all to be lost by advertising one's actions. This is where the old saying 'cast ye not pearls before swine' comes into play. If you tread this path carefully, then others of similar service are put in your path to work with. If you become stuck in the dead end, it forms into a stronger messiah trap and the whole 'illuminati of the modern age' bullcrap rears its head.

Each rung has its own steps within it that expose our weaknesses and strengths, and the rungs flow in a natural power manifestation rather than being imposed by human structures. The groups and lodges often have their own lessons, but in truth, life itself places the more powerful traps at your feet to see how you handle them. Power has a way of working and it will flow regardless of how we try to shape, funnel or use it. By taking a lone path, the initiate essentially hands over the lessons to be learned to a higher teacher and it can take a very strong sense of focus and self-examination to be able to walk the lone path. It is harder but infinitely more productive.

2

The Pitfalls
and
Traps of Magic

Oath taking

Once the neophyte is crossing the road to become an initiate, one of the first major issues to raise its head regardless of whether the person is a member of magical group/lodge, or a sole practitioner is the issue of oath taking. There are many reasons why oaths are asked of a magician, and to be honest with you, most of the reasons are a load of bull. There are a small number of reasons to take oaths and a very limited list of whom that oath should be bound to. There tend to be three basic types of oaths, the oath to a group, the oath to a deity or power, and the oath to a landmass. Within those categories there are many variants and sub categories with enough red tape to keep you going for months.

The first basic type is the oath to a group/lodge/fellowship. This tends to cover secrecy, honor and obedience towards the group, the work, the leader or all three. I am personally very uncomfortable with such oaths as they are easily misused, often connected or attached to curses, and are not really necessary. If there is work being done in the group that is of a nature that is best not discussed, one would hope that magicians working at that level would have enough intelligence to hold their tongues without pain of death. If such an oath is needed, it reflects the weakness of the group and therefore they should not be doing such work anyhow. If the oath is sworn to the leader, then it is very possible that there is the potential for a power grab going on where the leader is manipulating the members. Oaths are often asked for when there is something to hide - remember that.

Another unhealthy reason for oaths is an age-old adherence to drama and intrigue. It puts the members in a 'special status', a secret society, a brotherhood. That's all well and good if you are 18 years old but if you are a mature magician it is not really appropriate. When we come to the issue of magical knowledge that should be withheld, kept secret and preserved, the path of oath taking, I feel, is still not justified. Those who are unprepared at an inner level cannot understand magical knowledge. It reveals itself to a seeker only when the seeker is ready to receive it fully. Some naturally talented people can unravel magical texts and usually promptly blow themselves up. But the taking of oaths under these circumstances can be very unhealthy both for the practitioner and the magic itself.

The other very important issue regarding oath taking is that it disengages the individual's important learning curve regarding knowing when to keep silent and when not. The institutionalization of magical learning over the centuries has created a framework whereby the individual is not allowed to develop their own self-discipline, their own inner strength nor are they given space to develop individually at their own pace. When someone who is immature begins a path of practice that will potentially take them to strength, knowledge and power, they will show off and brag about it to their peers who are not involved in such a path. Life will teach such a person a lesson of maturity, which will be painful and embarrassing if they are perceptive.

If they are not perceptive, but are self-absorbed, they will continue to expose themselves to ridicule as they parade their path like a new coat. That will trap them magically at that stage and they will not travel much beyond the basics.

As the initiate matures, they usually become very aware that it is pointless to try and discuss magic outside of the community of magicians. Their silence becomes self-imposed. As the initiate progresses onto being an adept, they begin to see how magic is just another name for what is basically the power of the universe. That power is addressed in terms of religion, magic, physics and biology etc. When the adept talks about magic to a priest, or a theoretical physicist for example, it is very possible to have in depth magical conversations where you realize you are both talking about the same power, but you are both just using a different vocabulary. Hence the need for secrecy falls away. It's all about discernment, which is one of the major necessities in magic.

And this is why, for me personally, I have no qualms about writing certain texts and making them available: the lack of secrecy ensures that the information goes where it needs to. It is then possible for a physicist to pick up the work, read it, and recognize what it is that is being written about. Moving the vocabulary to one side, it is all about how power expresses itself through substance, and how you can actively be a part of that. The rules and regulations that abound in magical groups/lodges are outdated and follow a mentality of control and hierarchy. We need to move a little beyond and mature spiritually.

The other pitfall with oaths is the inner impact or binding that can affect the spirit and life path. Some magical oaths are constructed to be more than just a promise - they can become ritual binds that will trigger curses if that oath is broken. Sometimes, many times in fact, neophytes or new initiates are bound by ritual oaths to obedience and secrecy. Then they discover that the group or lodge is corrupt and is involved in magical practice that goes against the ethics of the individual. The ritual oath means the person who is oath bound cannot warn others, challenge the behavior or seek support, however confidential. It puts the individual in an ethically difficult situation in that they can potentially become silent witnesses to all manner of magical abuses. The side effect of such a curse bound oath is that they also become complicit in the unbalanced act and take on some of the energetic interplay that is tied to the ritual actions. Leaving the group is not enough to sever the oath, so it pays to be very choosy about what oaths one takes and to whom.

Deities rarely ask for heavy oaths, but it does happen, usually to the lone practitioner. This is because when you are not involved in a group, you are not in the middle of a power network that has hierarchies, so you are free to commune with whatever beings you choose. A lone practitioner will at some point be asked by a deity or a power to commit to a service or union for a limited time. You can simply agree or disagree to such a request, or one can swear an oath. Be very mindful that if you swear an oath, you cannot back out without repercussions.

The tying in of energy

This is something that most people do not realize when they attach themselves to a magical path, group or deity, and that is by partaking of that path, you are in effect tying yourself energetically to that path. That can happen naturally or can be imposed upon you. It happens naturally when you begin to work with a specific God or Goddess, your energies become interwoven with the magical interface that allows that power to interact with humanity. The more energetically sensitive you are, the deeper the impact upon your spirit will be. The same happens naturally when you work on a piece of land for a very long time, particularly if you also live on that land – you become entwined with its energy structure. This was the mechanism that was used in times past to accommodate sleepers within the land. It strengthens the interconnection with the land, and the power of the land flows through the practitioner as they mature in magical knowledge and skills.

The tying in of energy is also done intentionally when people join some magical lodges or groups. Their energies become connected, usually by way of initiation or oath, to the egregore and the magical structure that upholds the group. This can become extremely unhealthy as the balance of the whole structure is only as balanced as the person or persons upholding the group. Any action initiated by the leader is energetically tied to all its members so that the members in effect fuel the action. If this is done with consent, then all well and good, and people sometimes learn hard lessons. If this is done without consent, as is often the case, then irreparable damage can potentially be inflicted upon the energetic systems of the people. Most often this action without consent is done without bad intent, and sometimes without understanding, but nevertheless the results can take many years to untangle.

Because of these types of pitfalls and problems, it is wise to not get into oaths until you are absolutely sure what it is that you are getting involved in. It pays to look from an inner as well as an outer point of view, and if a person is not able to do that, then that in itself is an indication that oaths should not be taken. As for the tying in of energies, it is prudent to develop one's energy sensitivity as a priority when working/learning magical skills. With a heightened level of sensitivity, it is harder for a 'tying in' of energy to be imposed upon you, and the more ground foundation work one does the more solid the practitioner becomes. With that solidity comes boundaries, which are of paramount importance in magic. Without boundaries, one is quickly drained of energies in a variety of ways, and can be potentially exposed to powers that can seriously unbalance a sensitive mind. Anyone who walks a magical path must understand from the very beginning that you are ultimately responsible for yourself and you are not going to be protected from the results of your own bad decisions.

If you are walking a solitary path, the rules are the same. Inner contacts can initiate all the same problems that outer groups can, and one should proceed with caution and common sense at all times. The solitary path is something that does have less in the way of pitfalls, but is much harder to walk. The development however of a solitary magician is often fused with far more power than a group path if the solitary magician has good inner and outer boundaries, and lashings of self-discipline.

Blockage of knowledge

This is a favorite form of power manipulation in groups and lodges. The leader or 'inner court' members effectively block the neophytes and initiates from accessing certain lines of power 'for their own good'. I find this arrogant and elitist. There is nothing wrong in unraveling training in steps and ensuring that each person develops a strong foundation and good working practice. That is different. When someone who is being grounded in the foundations of magic, and they have natural talent, or have done this at some 'other time', the foundation training will awaken certain things within their consciousness which will allow them to access deeper inner realms and contacts. This is the hallmark of a true initiate: they find the inner keys for themselves. Many lodges hold very tight control over inner contacts and inner temples, locking out all but a few adepts, the chosen ones, which in effect mummifies the line of magic. This disengages the natural development of progress within the initiate ranks and keeps them disempowered. The result is a group of initiates who cannot access new realms and new contacts for themselves, and who often cannot step beyond the 'allowed' contacts. Such controlling behavior is degenerate and unforgivable.

The other form of blocking power that can happen in groups is where all the members are deliberately blocked from accessing the inner worlds in any way other than what is given to them. This can be done by giving the initiates certain meditations or visions to do that effectively block them from inner worlds and contacts. It is often done furtively, and in a way that would not arouse suspicion. I have personally witnessed an Eastern 'Lama' giving out a group meditation that was designed to stop the practitioner accessing power from the land. People trusted his robes and gentle smile and did not stop to think for a moment what it was they were doing. I was appalled by the arrogance of the man, that he did not even try to hide what he was doing, but instead sugar coated it with New Age sweetness.

Thankfully such behavior is not widespread and most blocking happens when the teacher feels 'justified'. I don't feel that there is such a justification; such 'nannying' of an initiate stops them from learning important lessons. Many initiates who are not strong enough to handle deeper inner contacts often cannot get them anyhow. If they are able to make the contacts but are not grounded enough to work with them, they will either shut down naturally, or they will fragment physically or mentally. Such power blocking is there to stop that from happening. But I do feel that, in the long-term pattern of spiritual development, it is an important phase to go through. By protecting a person from their actions, their natural inner evolution is suppressed and they do not really learn why not to do something. If they have been warned, that is enough, they have to make the choice, not the lodge. I have found that when the work begins to really pick up pace and the power levels rise, people who would be unsuitable for the work suddenly cannot get to the meetings. The inner contacts that are being worked with usually filter out unsuitable candidates, and they tend to be better judges than I so I trust that filtering.

The blocking of power for a solitary practitioner is not really an issue, as there is no one there to block him. If the lone practitioner is not capable of handling a contact, they will not get that contact. If one is being blocked from getting into somewhere or making contact with an inner being, it is usually because the inner 'do not disturb' sign is up for a reason. To this day, I sometimes find that I cannot access something, or sometimes I am booted out of the inner worlds. Usually within 24 hours I find out why – I would have an infection, or have energy building up for something else to be done, or there was something unhealthy going on and I was being filtered out of it. The more we work without outer imposed structure, the more we are guided in a healthier way by the inner world contacts and the natural tides of magic.

Past lives and Genetic Threads

Something that rears its head very quickly in magical training is the issue of past lives, ancient souls and blood lines. In our modern world of disconnected communities and disempowered people, it has a wonderful allure to hearken back to another life/personality/time when things were different. For a weaker personality, this can provide a refuge from the real world, where a person can be 'something' of importance.

It is important right from the outset to be able to distinguish reality from fantasy and the lines can very easily get blurred. Yes magic will exhume past living experiences, yes it will wake up other times when you have lived and yes it will also kickstart genetic knowledge held in your blood (along with feuds, quests and unfinished business). But such awakening has to be approached very carefully and with a level head. 'Past' is not 'better', it is just a memory that can be useful or not.

The mechanism of remembering 'past living' experiences in magic is to enable you to access magical knowledge that you acquired in other lives so that you can integrate that learning in a present day setting and use it consciously - that way you are not constantly re learning about the wheel. So before I go on to talk about how such memories can be used in magic, let's look at what can go wrong, and often does.

When people begin to reach back through time, or the magic awakens old dormant memories and skills, how that person reacts to the awakening will decide whether or not that person moves any further along the path of true magic. It is one of the swirls that catch people on the climb up the ladder of magical training and like so many other swirls, they can be spectacular in their presentation. The amount of people who get trapped at this phase and think they are Akhenaton, John Dee, Crowley, Dion Fortune etc is just mind-boggling. They spend the rest of their lives trying to recreate a past that never existed, or to live in a past culture that has no real relevance in today's world.

Who cares if you were John Dee in another life? You are not now, so get over it.

Past memories can do many things when they emerge, and the first thing to be wary of is getting into the glamour and drama of another life. It does not matter who you were, all that matters is the skill set that you have access to, awareness of any outstanding patterns that need to be addressed (and I mean magically, not psychologically) and any ongoing jobs. The ongoing jobs are not usually something that emerges early on in a magical training. The deep timeless consciousness of the soul only usually brings that to the fore when it is finally time to get back to work, and that can often be many years into the magical life of someone.

Access to the magical skill set is often the first thing to emerge from other lives. The skills initially emerge unconsciously and will have been triggered by the practitioner's involvement in a situation that demands such a skill. So you are put in a situation that is new to you in this life, but you will feel like you are slipping into a comfy old favorite pair of slippers. You will be on home turf and will be able to access things you didn't know that you knew. When that happens, it is best to expand that opening by going into silence through meditation, so that it can emerge naturally. Sometimes, the door can be opened by a specific event, but what comes after that needs to be approached with care and intelligence. Powers and skills need to emerge in their own time without being forced and if the ground is prepared by stillness and meditation, and an 'openness' to allow nature to do her job, then the skills will emerge as needed.

An example. When I was a youngster, a man called Dr Gupta, a doctor in Bradford who was running a small research project, hypnotized me. I regressed quickly which was not expected or intended, and the major thing to come out of it for me was the emergence of the void. I was talked into a space 'between lives' where I was still, silent and in a place of profound power. I did not have the vocabulary to properly verbalise what I was experiencing, but the experience itself stayed with me and changed me forever. It opened the doors within me, and skills started to spill out. They came out slowly though, emerging over a twenty-year period that allowed me to properly integrate them and build upon them. I never consciously at any point tried to actively engage the skill memory, which to be honest with you is something that never occurred to me anyway during those years. I tended to bumble my way through things, blissfully unaware most of the time of what the hell was going on around and even within me.

If you do try to actively engage the memories, they filter through your present day mental vocabulary and you can quickly get trapped in the 'story' as opposed to engaging the skills you actually need. Anything that you try to force under such circumstances will shut down upon you as power just does not flow like that. Magical development in general has a basic rule - focus on what is directly in your path and the rest of it falls into place as you go.

Outstanding patterns are things that begin to emerge as the magical development of the individual progresses. By outstanding patterns I mean events that play out, often mirroring mythical patterns that are much bigger than ourselves. So I am not talking particularly about personal behavior patterns, but rather patterns of power that play out through families, lodges, races and cultures. When we recognize what is happening we can choose to get back on the hamster wheel of the pattern or we can opt to look for more imaginative solutions to our small part in the play —what can we do to change the cycle for the better?

Often recognizing a pattern and consciously deciding not to partake of it is enough to break the cycle. The most common patterns are ones of war/conflict/magical infighting and rival temple powers. To dive back in to 'do your bit', or 'defend the ancestors' adds to the pattern, which feeds power to all the beings that have a vested interest in keeping the pattern going. One of the maturing factors of magical development is the conscious decision to find better more balanced ways to resolve your part in the pattern. By focusing on your own actions, you allow the deeper powers to run through the pattern as a whole. Often the best action is not actually a part of the pattern, but a small regular act of service to uphold or help the beings that are working within the fate pattern. This in turn is mirrored in the magical development of the adept who finally gets to a stage of realizing that most of the time, magic is not the appropriate action. The longer and deeper you do magic, the less you do – it becomes very clear that most of the time is it just interfering with a bigger pattern. This is why certain lines of adepts choose unconditional magic in service: you turn up, lend a helping hand and then leave without ever knowing what the hell you just did. That way, it is very hard to interfere or impose your own opinioned action upon a situation.

Candy shop magic

This is a term I use for the practice of buying into any and all magical paths, books, courses, workshops, outfits and silly jewelry/haircuts/t shirts. The person hops from one book to another, from one path to another, constantly looking for the next power fix and glamour image. One week it's Chumbley, the next it's Fortune, Enochian magic, Egyptian magic and so on. I am not saying that someone should stick with one path because that is equally unhealthy. But there needs to be a sensible solid consistency in the initial learning so that something can take root and begin to grow. We have to learn the rules before we can break them. This is obvious to anyone who has studied any classical discipline to a professional level. Once you know one system of work well from the inside out, then you can throw that structure away if needs be and access virtually anything that is even remotely on the same frequency. So lodge secrecy regarding contacts becomes obsolete: once you have worked in depth with inner contacts, you can access just about anyone or anything. You don't need to have the contacts handed to you: just go get them for yourself.

If you are a lone practitioner, it is even better though it is harder. The lone practitioner needs to find an initial training mechanism that will teach inner and outer pattern making, provide boundaries and self-discipline. It takes a lot more work because it all has to come from within you, but it is far more rewarding if you achieve it and certainly more powerful. You also do not end up with the sometimes-ridiculous rules, poor quality work and low level dross that often accompanies beginner training.

Once that basic foundation is there and inner contacts have been made and worked with, then it becomes interesting to go and look at these various systems. The truths and flaws quickly become apparent in a way that would not have been so obvious in the early stages of the initiate. That way, you can read interesting ideas, be challenged, informed and view all of them with a critical eye. There is too much written about magic by people who have no real inner experience. They rely on other books, history, philosophy and myths to come to their conclusions, rather than direct experience. A beginner would not realize that is what is happening, but an initiate who has experience of deeper inner work will immediately spot the flaws in the text and move swiftly on.

The other problem with candy shop magic is that the various paths that are dived in and out of often don't mix well, and from a power point of view can be antagonistic. So mixing deities that are not connected, with a form of magic that is not connected to them can result in anything from total failure to a power kickback that unbalances the practitioner. Ever wondered why so many chaos magicians suffer from depression? Yes, power does have the potential to work in such a way, but only when done with a deep and full knowledge of the ingredients that are being put together. A trained classical musician, for example, can write a crazy piece of orchestrated music using unusual instruments and make it work...why?, because they know how the rules of sound works. Someone who is just messing about with instruments and can sort of play one enough to busk is not quite the same. The outcome will most probably be noise. The same goes for power and magic. Learn the deep rules first, then push the boundaries.

Glamour, Control and Ego

The three 'magic' words. These are the biggest of all of the pitfalls. Magical paths and individual teachers can present themselves in a very glamorous way. They draw power around themselves, people look up to them and they begin to behave like rock stars. They then start to try and control their adoring 'fans' with rules and demands which in turn feeds their ego. Groups similarly shroud themselves in secrecy, club rules and ranks. They appear as mysterious and have goals that you are told you may be able to aspire to, but will possibly never reach...guaranteed to draw an audience.

A wide-eyed young aspirant sees what they perceive as power and begin to emulate so that the next generation of egomaniacs is ready and waiting. It's the same pattern as cult behavior and people fall for it all the time. They get away with really bad behavior because people will turn a blind eye and more often than not, they will try to excuse or even to copy such behavior.

This weeds out the idiots from powerful magic and keeps them in magical primary school. If you are starting out on a magical path either with a group or alone and you find yourself adoring some teacher/leader/adept… remember one thing – their shit stinks just the same as yours. And if they are playing on the glamour, they are probably not quite as powerful as they would have you think. Power does not need glamour. Power is hard work, like chopping wood. It burdens people with responsibility, it challenges them and their actions on a daily basis, and then it puts you to work.

So when you approach a magical path, do not disengage your common sense: use the same early warning alarm systems you do in every day life. Do not believe everything you see and are told - personal experience is everything in magic, and never ever hand over your power or will to someone else.

3
Power
and
Magic

Magic is about working with power - it is the calling of power, the manipulation of power and the moving of power from A to B. The forms that we work with in vision and ritual, the names, beings and objects are just vessels for the power; they are also just matrices that allow interface between conscious power and humanity. It is very important to understand this when walking a magical path: it is all power and nothing more.

When we first tread a magical path we are often swept up in a tide of rituals, beings, magical objects, visionary inner worlds and inner contacts. Our conscious mind is kept busy with the 'inner' reality show and that allows our minds to interface with Universal Power. But the clutter of human magic, the accoutrements, is just a dressing that presents itself until our consciousness becomes malleable enough to work without such dressing. Eventually the work becomes a wordless formless movement of power that has no defined goal other than pure inner instinct: we become a conscious part of the Universal Power. But a practitioner of magic has to go through the stages to get to such instinctive work; through the structure the magician finds the nature of power. Why? Because that is how our consciousness works.

Boundaries

The first skill that is paramount when working with power is boundaries. If you have no boundaries for the magic, it will over take you and destroy you. Another word for the boundaries is frequencies. When you work in a particular magical stream, you connect to a certain 'frequency' of magic so that when you are correctly tuned to that frequency you only pick up what is a part of that path. This is very important because such defined tuning blocks out many unhealthy inner beings, realms etc that could be parasitical or damaging. It allows the magician to learn and grow in a relatively safe environment. The longer that path has been walked, the more tuned and focused it is, the safer it becomes. Such boundaries can be self-imposed for a new magician learning alone providing it is approached with careful thought.

The boundaries themselves present as self-imposed restrictions on what action is taken, what element of power is worked with and what inner visions are done. Add to that, the regular daily exercise of grounding and stabilizing meditations and the potential magician is on the right path. The restricted path should be a longer term endeavor, not a two week burst of enthusiasm that quickly vanishes.

So for example, a person wishes to train themselves in magic. After learning the very basics of the directions and observing what is around them, they would choose one direction with one element and begin to work with it. From a visionary point of view there would be one place, usually a place of learning like the inner library, where they would go in vision on a weekly basis. There would be one simple ritual that is done regularly until its power begins to flow, and a daily meditation to train and discipline the mind.

The simple vision or ritual often gets cast to one side in search of something more powerful and interesting, and such action is a dead end that pulls the prospective magician off the tracks. Some of the simplest rituals are the most powerful once the magician has learned the deeper frequency of the ritual and can interact with it. For me, the most powerful ritual of all is the lighting of the candle. It opens all worlds, all times and gives me access to focused power that is unfiltered. Boundaries contain the power so that it begins to build, allowing the new practitioner to slowly adjust physically to being in the presence of power.

The inner vision of the library has a bit more freedom to a budding magician because all of the books in the library are in fact the consciousness of many magicians and priests/esses throughout time. It is possible to interact with these wise minds and learn a great deal. Working within the visionary confines of the library allows the spirit to interact with inner contacts in a variety of ways while still maintaining boundaries.

So the combination of a daily simple stillness meditation, a twice weekly ritual working with a specific element in a specific direction, and twice weekly visits to the inner library is a good foundation training that will seriously build inner muscle over a year. Working to such restriction over a year will build the inner battery for power and will give the practitioner a solid basic foundation to work from. During that first year, it would be wise to not read tons of magical books, but to work with a small selection that is within the same field. It is important that the ritual and visionary experiences of the practitioner in the early stages of training are not influenced by the writing of others; it is vitally important that the reading is done after the experiences, not before.

The other very important and often overlooked boundary that is needed to work with power is a physical discipline. That can take the form of anything from a physical training like martial arts, dance, athletics etc to disciplines like dietary restrictions, yoga etc. It is also good to do a regular physical service whether that entails tending a patch of land, looking after a few graves of local ancestors or gardening for an elderly neighbor. Doing something that sometimes you do not want to do, but have to, is very good for self-imposed boundaries. Service is very important in magic as it teaches us not to be selfish; a quality that is not good to mix with power. The physical discipline builds up strength and enables the body to process large amounts of power, and the service builds stamina. With strength and stamina the power can flow unfettered through a human and be mediated to whatever situation needs it.

Working with Power

If someone just wants to dress up in the outfits, wave around wands and utter silly incantations, then power will never be an issue for them. If however a prospective magician truly wants to know how to engage power, work through the worlds and interact with the many beings of the inner realms, then they really need to learn how to interact intelligently with power.

Once a magician has learned how to connect with power, they need to know what to do with it and how to do it: a common mistake that people make when dealing with power is that they identify themselves with it and take it on as a mantle. This quickly leads to messiah or magus syndrome where they put themselves on a pedestal and quickly self-destruct: they become parodies of what they aspire to. Some also try to power grab, i.e. hold on to the power themselves and not let others engage freely with it. That also brings about degeneration and the inner worlds eventually disengage from such individuals.

Those are the most common mistakes. The subtler ones to watch for are where the power begins to fragment parts of the mind and/or body that are not able to hold such power. This can happen through willful stupidity or blissful ignorance. If someone is ill and does not realize, and they work with a high level of power, the power will find the weak point in the body and smash it wide open. It will do the same to any emotional or mental weakness or frailty: hence the need to be physically and mentally solid before working with higher levels of power.

Loss of Ego

This is a very important step in the path to working with magical power, and that is the ability to loosen the grasp on the ego. This is talked about frequently, often in very philosophical terms, in a variety of spiritual and magical traditions. Such traditions often take it too far so that people are expected to lose the very essence that defines them in magic.

To lose the ego in a healthy way means to have conscious awareness of what a small player you truly are in a very big show, and when you get a taste of power, to understand that to connect with such power is actually normal – it does not mean you are 'chosen' or 'special'. By understanding this, the next step, which is to drop the need to control, is far easier to swallow. Surrendering control of a situation is a major step in working with large amounts of power, because without such surrender, the power cannot truly flow. We limit ourselves by our need to contain power and make it do what we want it to. Our imaginations and ability to look at the longer range prospect of an action is so limited that we cannot possibly mediate the full flow of power and contain it. We end up in a losing battle with nature and the forces that flow all around us. And when those forces do things we do not like and we cannot control, we label them as evil. Such behavior is a pattern within humanity that rears its head from the smallest issue to the biggest project.

But by relinquishing control, we then have to approach power either unconditionally, or in harmony with everything else. When we step beyond the toddler phase of 'it's all about us', we then begin to see how these vast powers which can be horrifically destructive, are also regenerative and are just doing their jobs. The same goes for smaller powers that flow through magic: when they flow in balance, regardless of their outcome, we must learn to live with and around that power, rather than contain or manipulate it.

A good example of this is the tale of Lilith. This power, which is a hive consciousness, is the force of storms in the desert, which often brings with it death to the weak. This power, identified in some desert cultures as female, and in others as male, also began to be connected in Near Eastern myths with parasitical powers that induced sexual dreams in God fearing Jewish men (it was her, they cry, I didn't do anything...yeah right). Some of that connection is a construct used to keep that power from being communed and worked with. Such rewriting of powers has potential to be a book in itself – it was frequently done, and still is, to keep people away from raw power. Back to Lilith. So that power of storms and death became feared, reviled, and 'amulets a many' were created to keep her/them/it at bay. But no-one ever stops to ask what true function that power has in our world?

The power of the storms is about keeping the land healthy. So instead of battling the storms with magic, how about learning to live with such storms in a healthy way? How about learning about its power and working with it in service? By doing so, the magician learns to attune to the power and can feel it coming: he will feel its intention, its path, its force and will be able to act accordingly. Such a magical connection with the land and power was adeptly displayed by the Andaman Island's Aboriginal Indians, who live on a string of islands in the Indian Ocean. When the tsunami hit, they were already safely tucked away at the top of the hills. They moved hours before the giant wave hit. They were in tune with the land and talked to the sea. They knew the earthquake was coming and they knew the sea was coming, so they got out of the way.

So back to the Near East. Instead of working with the power of the storms, and the call of death at the door of a newborn, which is about genetic health and ensuring there is no overpopulation, the people worked against that power. Lilith was presented as a female demon, she was reviled, hated, and vast numbers of people prayed against her. Magical amulets kept that power at bay and other powers were prayed to, in an effort to stop the storms: a magical battle of wills began that continues in our psyche to this day. How much simpler it would have been to acknowledge the power of the storms and live/work around them, and to take responsibility for population control and genetic health so that land powers did not need to do that for us. The Andaman islanders have proved that it works. They live as our ancient ancestors did; in harmony, in balance, with very little disease. They are truly living in the Garden.

It's all about keeping the balance. When you begin to work magically with deeper powers such issues will come to the fore and we have to be very careful indeed to ensure that we are working with the power in a balanced way, not in a selfish or egotistical way that will strengthen and encourage imbalance. It's about changing how we think about power. If we take the time to watch, listen and learn, the powers of nature have incredible lessons to teach us about how power works and what our parts are in such power displays. Most of the jobs of a magician are about restoring balance - very simple, very unglamorous and not very useful if you want to get laid or have a new car.

Power Drunkenness

One of the major dangers of doing high magic without foundations, without scruples and without commonsense, is the 'all singing all dancing' spectacular 'blowing a fuse'. If someone has natural ability and they play with powerful magical rituals or visions, they will get a possible hit. If they have no boundaries or foundation, or they approach it with a lust for power, then they will get blown apart.

When people get a first taste of real magic, if there is no internal discipline within the practitioner it can be like a drug. Such a taste becomes an addiction and magic is done just because they can do it, to prove something to themselves, to impress others or to draw things to them. When they succeed, the ego becomes inflated and the common sense goes out of the window. Just as amphetamine can give people a false sense of importance and greatness, so can magical power. It will hike you up on a great high and you will plateau before you crash unceremoniously to the ground. The crash can come in the way of degeneracy, idiocy, or mental instability. It can be fast and spectacular or it can be slow and insidious, but it will come one way or the other. History is littered with tales of magicians degenerating slowly into rotting heaps, literally blowing themselves up, or becoming parodies of themselves.

But what causes the power drunkenness in the first place? Weakness in the personality. Everyone has a weakness of some sort or another, which is not really the problem. What does cause the problem is when there is a weakness in the body, mind or personality and the person does not address it. It is ignored, denied, dodged and compensated for, which points to someone who is not ready to know himself. And that takes us back to the words the initiates read as they enter the sanctum: *Man, Know Thyself*.

If you have a weakness, and you are aware of it, then you take that weakness into account when you begin to work on something magically. If you know that weakness will interfere with a magical job, then you withdraw and wait until you are stronger. Just being aware of a weakness goes a long way towards dealing with it. We all have them without exception; the trick is to know what they are and what you have to do to compensate for that weakness. This takes us back to the self-discipline issue that is one of the earliest lessons in the magical path and one of the most important qualities in a magician. If you know your weakness, and you focus on addressing it while also walking a magical path, then power drunkenness will not be a major issue.

In the end, how we approach power dictates how we will approach magic and in turn how that magic will affect us, and everything around us. This is why the initial path of magical training or self-learning should be slow and precise: get those feet firmly planted in the earth and remember how much it hurts if you stick a wet metal fork into a plug socket.

The Power Dynamics of Ritual and Vision

A major question for beginning and experienced magicians alike is, when do you use inner powers, when do you use outer patterns and when do you simply cause an effect by observation or participation? There are no easy answers to such questions and I feel that there is no real hard fast 'rule' to make such decisions clearer. It all depends on the person, situation and intent. The more you immerse yourself in a magical life, the more fluid and 'chameleon like' such a path becomes. Humanity makes hard fast rules and hits such barriers like a truck traveling at high speed. In real terms, the universe is an ever changing, diverse and confounding power that is infinitely harmonious.

A major key to working with inner powers is the ability to adapt and change, to be able to question the rules and to follow instincts. It is important to understand that most outer ritual will not really work well without the inner plug stuck in the socket: without inner fuel they become psychologised rituals and 'feel good' imaginary actions. Such inner fuel comes from either a person's natural mediating abilities or their trained skills in visionary magic.

There are cases however where pre constructed rituals that have been used before with inner power, will work properly when performed without any inner connection. When a ritual is 'contacted', it becomes a single beacon of power. After that, if the ritual is repeated exactly, it is connected back to the original ritual: they become one and the same action. The ritual passes through time and every time the ritual is performed, it is manifesting the original ritual with all its contacted power. This is why ancient rituals, when conducted exactly to the prescribed pattern, will work. What is happening is not a re enactment, or a repeat of, it is a reconnecting to the original ritual so that its power continues down through time. This was understood and demonstrated very well in ancient Egypt; they knew that a certain ritual had to be exact, with the original tools, words, timing etc. That is because they knew that performing the ritual in this way brought the original ritual, with all its contacted beings and power, through time and up to their present day.

Maintaining ritual this way ensured that the power and structure stayed in place and that the ritual would work even if there were a generation of priests who had no contact ability. If they did everything in the ritual as they should, the contact would work because the ritual would be passing through time and connecting to the original. This was also very important because the preparation involved in opening a power contact, and the energy needed to maintain that contact, would have been massive. The rituals were not minor issues; they maintained the rivers, the weather, the birth of new generations and the health of the crops. If any of these failed, then the population would die. So the rituals had to draw in deities and associated beings that had the power to work in harmony with such flows of nature. To manifest that level of contact, with multiple deities over a year cycle was an incredible amount of work. There is no way that such rituals could be done from scratch year in and year out as the pressure would wipe out the priesthood.

The way to get around such a problem is to ensure that the contacted ritual could travel through time; so it would need to be re triggered year after year. To take the ritual through time with its contacts, it had to be repeated exactly, with the same tools, same words, same everything. Then it became joined with the original; the power and contact would flow through time and through the repeated action. The patterns of those rituals are still imprinted in the inner worlds and can be awoken with the right skills and tools. In today's world, the same technique can be used; once a contacted ritual is created, it can be revisited if re created exactly.

Using Inner Power

The foundation training in vision/astral work opens the consciousness up to the deeper powers that run through magic, enabling the power to flow through the inner landscape of the practitioner. The deeper into the inner realms a magician goes, the less intricate the rituals need to be. The human consciousness becomes more fluid through visionary work, allowing the mind to stretch out and interconnect with all the patterns of power that flow around the outer world. Once the mind becomes comfortable and able to handle the stretches of worlds and power, it slowly becomes entwined in the inner patterns; this is the 'plugging in' phase of visionary magic. It can take anything from a couple of years to many years to achieve this, depending on how flexible and stable the practitioner is. The mind needs to be disciplined and yet unfettered at the same time. Once that stage is reached, wherever the mind goes, power truly follows.

So let's break this down a little. The steps towards accessing inner power are simple and very hard work. First the mind must be disciplined, and then the imagination must be loosened. From there, once the basic ability is in place, the practitioner needs to learn about how they individually perceive the over all structure of the inner worlds. Many books have been written over the years about how many astral planes there are, what color they are etc, but in reality, the living breathing universe is not quite that accommodating. Things are not so neat and tidy, hence the need to be flexible, and to not be indoctrinated before you get your feet off the ground. The best writings to read about the inner worlds and attendant angelic beings, are The

Revelations of John of Patmos, The Book of Ezekiel and other visionary ancient texts. What you are reading in those visions is a true glimpse as to the reality of the strangeness of inner power. They are not allegories, or hints; they are direct descriptions that are literal: the mysteries are indeed hidden within the text!

The first stage of visionary/astral work, once the basic skills are in place, is the connection with humanity's stored knowledge and interface with divinity. Humanity's stored knowledge is what the Theosophists called the Akashic records and what others call the Great Library. It is the consciousness of all learning that has been done by humanity and it is the wisdom and knowledge of those who have gone before. It is also a filter for new understanding flowing out of the void – it passes through the library before flowing into the minds of those ready to receive it. Where does that new knowledge come from? To be honest with you I haven't a bloody clue.

In the Great Library, what we perceive as books, scrolls etc are in fact fragments of magicians, priests/priestesses, scholars, inventors, healers etc. The part of them that held the knowledge in life was jettisoned at their death and passed into the Great Library. If you wish to learn something of depth, that is where you go. It is also a place where one can access many different temples throughout time, various inner adepts and a variety of streams of magic and religion. All those threads come together in this powerful place of learning and wisdom.

This is why it is a good thing for a new practitioner to spend at least the first year of their training simply going into the library and making contact with the teachers and their various skills. Often an inner adept will put a book 'into' you, which means they have connected you to the knowledge and teacher that is that book. Its lessons will slowly unfold over the years and that is one of the major keys to the library: you don't go pick up a book, read it and go, oh! The books flow into you and unravel in their own time. It can take anything from a few weeks to many years. I am still unraveling things I was plugged into back in the early 90s.

The progression from the Great Library is usually a natural one. The practitioner is guided from the library to other places, usually inner patterns of outer temples and from there they are slowly introduced to the various realms and beings. This is the greatest form of education as it is solely the responsibility of the magician to direct their own learning, and it is coming from inner sources, not outer classes or programs. The practitioner occasionally gets outer confirmation of their inner training when they come across a book in the outer world that talks about what they have experienced on the inner. It is always far better to get it yourself through inner discovery and then have outer confirmation, than to learn from a book or outer teacher and have to take their word for it. Go find out for yourself!

The period of active visionary work can take quite a few years and there is no real way of speeding that process up. It will take however long it needs to take. From that solid visionary aspect, it will slowly become apparent that you can slip into inner realms quickly and without vision, just by thinking about them. This is where the inner and outer minds are coming together and the consciousness is becoming fluid. During this phase, the practitioner flows between solid inner visions, interacting with beings in vision, and simply thinking about them and being there. Again this phase will take as long as it needs to take and will run parallel to similar developments in the ritual work which we will discuss in a minute.

The ability to be able to interact with an inner contact just by virtue of thinking about them is a very important phase as it demonstrates the ability of the magician to be able to truly hold themselves in more than one world at once. Having the body in one world and the mind in another is one thing, but having the mind in two places, interacting in both places at the same time is the stage whereby the inner powers are preparing to truly flow from outer to inner in a constant conversation of power. So in practical terms, a practitioner would be walking around a sacred site (or the supermarket) and could be holding a conversation with someone while also interacting with the power site, talking with the inner contacts there and also be interacting with the inner pattern of the sacred site. Balancing the mind going in so many directions at once is a key skill which takes many years of practice, and it quickly becomes very clear why anyone with mental instability should not do magic: they would fragment very quickly under such strain.

It is also at this phase where the inner vision and outer ritual come together. As the magician is walking around the temple conducting a ritual, so they are also walking in the inner worlds weaving the power and interacting with the inner beings that are connected with the ritual. The two actions work simultaneously and allow power to flow back and forth, manifest to un-manifest in a dance of power.

Outer Power/ritual

In magical practice, outer power mainly expresses itself through the use of ritual action. When a new practitioner begins to explore magic, the first thing they usually encounter is ritual. At first the ritual seems to be a dramatic action that bonds the group, focuses intention and attention, and specifies, through action, a magical intent. This layer of ritual was quickly taken up by psychologists and is used to unravel certain issues through action and intent.

The next layer of ritual that surfaces in magic is the layer by which the practitioner repeatedly assigns a certain direction, altar, object or statue a specific power and identity. This is the first step on the bridge to connecting with true outer power through ritual. The mental intent married to a ritual action kick starts the wheels of power into action and the power it produces heavily depends up either the mental focus of the practitioner or the embedded pattern of ritual in the object or direction.

An embedded pattern of ritual is an inner pattern that has built up over time, and engaging this pattern through magical action and intent will trigger the pattern regardless of the ability of the practitioner. It is a bit like a neuro-engram; a pattern/action repeated many times in exactly the same way will create specific memory pathways in the brain. Once that engram pattern is in place, the need for conscious action goes and the action becomes an automatic response. So it is with magical patterns repeated over generations in the same place and in the same way. The magical reaction of the ritual power moves from conscious to automatic. This was probably one of the reasons why, in many ancient temples that worked with high levels of magical power, only the highest initiates were allowed to access the inner court/ sanctum. This restriction stopped the idiots from waltzing in and pressing the red button.

It is interesting to note that in some ruins of ancient temples, these patterns are still operating. It is as if the temple was abandoned so quickly that the priests never had time to shut them down. Those who have the knowledge or keys to the ritual will still be able to operate the temple's magical power. Many other temples though are tightly shut and the ritual patterns have either been dismantled or are ritually sealed.

The next step on from working an engrammed ritual is a ritual of conscious engagement. This type of ritual relies heavily upon the visionary or inner response skills of the practitioner. A ritual of conscious engagement is where the practitioner works *through* the object or direction, through ritual action and speech, to connect with inner powers drawn in to assist with the ritual intent. So as a practitioner approaches a direction/altar, they call from an inner point of view as well as an outer point of view for the power or consciousness that they wish to work with. This is the first stage of vision and ritual coming together as a working method. So the outer ritual prepares the space and tunes the frequency needed, it puts the practitioner and /or objects in a certain pattern, and then uses vision to bridge inner power/contacts into the pattern so that the ritual is conducted on both inner and outer planes through direct intent and action. This is a very effective way to work that shares the burden of power out between the soul, mind and body. The patterned outer structure of the ritual takes up some of the impact and spreads the power out into a more manageable job.

High ritual

What I term as high ritual is not impressive scripts, velour robes and gold fabric headdresses (God forbid), but a form of ritual that is one of the highest frequency methods of working without blowing yourself up. In high ritual, there are many things going on at once and the practitioner has to carry burdens on many levels as they work. The outer ritual carries on as normal, but at the same time the practitioner is also doing the same outer ritual action in an inner temple in vision, while also mediating/interacting with power/contact/pattern in their own realm.

Any use of speech must be conducted while also talking to the inner contact/deity/power with the mind. At the same time the practitioner will be expected to conduct ritual action both in vision and in body. It can take many years to achieve this skill but the equal distribution between outer action and inner action is one of the least impacting ways of doing powerful work. It is working to the scales of balance but if large amounts of power are worked with, then both the mind and the body will take the impact.

Visionary action

This type of action is a step on from high ritual and is where the lines between vision and ritual completely merge and the spearhead of the action is intent. Visionary action needs a very pliable mind, a focused body and a deep familiarity with power. One of the hallmarks of powerful magic is that the more powerful the magic, the less formed the action/vision/ritual. So when your mind and body becomes truly comfortable with power, it has no need of elaborate rituals and visions to navigate through magic, instead it develops a sense of 'touch' for want of a better word, where everything moves in a natural way with a little stewarding. It is a bit like homeopathy or cranial osteopathy; a little conscious movement goes a long way.

So for example, calling in a power or deity is done in the ritual space by first standing very still and tuning into the rhythm of the space. The magician then reaches with the mind through the space for the rhythm of the power she wishes to draw in, and by using movement, reaches out both inwardly and outwardly to connect and flow with that power. It becomes a Tai Chi type motion where the body and mind flow like a river to commune and connect with power and consciousness. The intent governs everything, so it becomes an awareness of power with intent and nothing more. A physical motion interrupts the stillness of the tuned space, gathers the power and moves it by way of focused body movement. This is probably where the use of mudras arose when Indian dance style *Bharat Natyam* was still a form of ritual action and not a mere performance?

When the mind becomes tuned to this level of action, it can effect change or connection through the action of observation. Just as in quantum physics, observation alters the outcome of an experiment, so just 'being' with intent in a ritual space will effect change. The difference between the random effect in experiments of passive observation, and the directed intent, is that observing magic with focused intent gives a specific repeatable result. It is a controlled use of power to affect change rather than a random result from a passive action. The only pre requisite is the level of focus and magical experience in the person doing the observing. Without that level of experience, the observation simply elicits a random change from the human presence: the change cannot be directed or focused for a specific action or outcome.

This dynamic can be seen when a magician who has experience of inner and outer ritual visits a sacred site, temple, church or dramatic re enactment. The mere presence and observation by the magician alters the power pattern and brings about change. If the magician has no specified intent other that to acknowledge the power of the place, then the change will be unconditional, whatever is needed for the site, but it will not be random. If the magician observes with intent, then the intent will trigger specific powers into action. Hence the more experienced the magician is, the less they seem to do (and without velour robes and silly headdresses).

Inner worlds and actions: cause and effect

Usually when people embark upon a mission to learn and practice magic, they give little or no thought to what will be the long-term consequences. We have all been there in one form or another and most develop beyond that, but some do not. Some people do magic to get what they want and to control their universe, some people do magic to affect the world according to their agenda, some do magic because that is how they breathe, and some people have no clue why they do it, just that they are driven down a particular path and they go with the flow. All of these, plus many more reasons for doing magic have positive and negative effects on the individual and the worlds around them. I say worlds because magic not only affects the outer world, its ripples pass through all the worlds in one way or another.

Any act of magic will have an effect through the worlds to a greater or lesser degree, because magic is the tuning fork of the universe: it is the vibration that affects change far beyond our understanding of the original action and allows us to perceive and interact with power. Our very limited understanding of the universe prevents us from seeing the vast multi-layered highways of consciousness, power and substance (particles), how they interact and how their interactions trigger more highways, patterns and expressions. Just as we are all moving faster and away from ground zero of the big bang, so magic expands and accelerates from its initial action.

That is why when you do a simple magical act the first time it is weak. But over the years, as your consciousness strengthens and your ability to perceive subtler 'vibrations' from the tuning fork of the universe strengthens, so the re-visited act gets more and more complex. What is actually happening is that as the initial magical act expands and gets 'faster' as it moves away from the point of origin, so it grows, and as the magician re-visits that 'highway' of the magical act, they interface with an increasingly faster, more diffuse, more complex line of magic than they had originally initiated.

My personal deepest experience of that is with the lighting and tuning of the candle flame. The intent to light a candle to prepare the space for a ritual act developed from that simple stance, to an act of bringing into physical manifestation an elemental expression that lights through all worlds and all times: it becomes the light of divinity within everything. And that is the biggest clue to all magical acts: in its true expansion, all magic is an expression of the power of divinity. By divinity I do not mean deity, but the unexplainable ultimate conscious power of the universe. So when you meddle with such power, it bodes well to use a bit of foresight and commonsense.

So let's bring it a bit closer to home and look at it in more practical terms. The inner and outer worlds are not separate realms; they are intricately interwoven like a bolt of fine linen. Anything you do energetically in one realm affects many others. It's that simple. The action/reaction seesaw between the worlds is a strange and interesting one, and the way it all balances is very curious. Small focused actions create massive energetic responses. Large diffuse actions create little response. The more condensed the power, the heavier the result has to be to balance the seesaw. A beautiful example of that is the Tree of Life. The first three spheres balance out the rest of the seven spheres, that is because the first three have a stronger 'divine' power than the other seven which are basically continued expressions of the first three (if I were to put the Higgs Bosun particle aka the God particle, anywhere on the Tree, it would be with those three first spheres). The Tree is a good expression of the acceleration of magical/divine power as it expands, changes frequency and becomes more diffuse and complex. The tenth sphere is the fully externalized expression of power, i.e. our world, and beyond the tenth sphere are the actions of time (past, present, future).

So 'inner power' is denser energetically but has no physical expression of itself in our understanding of the laws of physicality, where as 'outer' power is more diffuse, has less density but has a stronger physical expression. Thus a small amount of inner power is balanced by a much bigger expression of outer power (with anti matter falling into the category of outer power, and dark matter being categorized as inner power).

The other thing that becomes obvious from a magical point of view is that there is not just inner and outer, there are many other layers of power in between that all interact with each other. In magical terms pure divine power is on one end of the seesaw and all expressions that come from that power are on the other. On the Tree of Life, it translates to three expressions of divinity that have issued from the pure inner power on one end of the seesaw and life/death/all of creation is on the other.

This translates in magical practical terms thus: a conscious interaction with a small amount of inner power creates a much bigger expression or reaction in the outer world. The closer to the source of the inner power you get, the more profound and powerful that interaction becomes, with long term consequences for the physical world. But it also depends upon the frequency that the magician is 'vibrating' at (remember the tuning fork of the universe?). So if you go back to the lighting of the candle it would go something like this.

The magician lights a candle with intent to tune a sacred space. The magician is in the early days of magical work, so he has not consciously interacted much with that 'tuning' fork/magic, therefore his 'vibration' is currently tuned to physicality more than anything. Therefore he does not perceive the real power behind the magical action – he cannot perceive the density of inner power in its pure form.

As the magician continues to interact with the magic away from the physical, i.e. in vision (no physical act), so his vibration begins to change as he moves his consciousness into non-physical realms. This allows him to perceive non-physical power and with that perception comes understanding that leads to more interaction in the inner worlds.

The more he practices lighting the candle, the more he begins to perceive the power as it moves away from the initial point of action, and the diffuse complexity of that power is seen and interacted with. This in turn builds momentum in the vibrational change of the magician, so it becomes a conscious interaction between the ever expanding magical inner power and the magician. Through that interaction, the consciousness of the magician begins to flow with that highway of power expression, and there comes a point when the magician can revisit or observe the initial expression of inner power triggered by the very first lighting of the candle. The magician is now vibrating at a frequency where he can fully perceive its power to the best of human ability. Hence the act becomes more and more profound, greater power is perceived, and the direct long term energetic consequence of the action is now observable. This is why magicians who work deeply in the inner realms do less and less magic as they mature, but when they do initiate a magical action, its long term effects can be considerable.

Justice, Balance and Karma

The minute one begins to walk a magical path and starts to interact and influence the 'tuning fork of the universe' that person takes on the responsibility of justice/karma. Why? Because a magical action has consequence and you bear responsibility for that.

These are words that do not often pop into the heads of people first walking a magical path, as the focus of intent is more often directed towards the acquisition of power, skill and peers. I have had interesting conversations with elderly occultists regarding the subject of justice/karma and I think the misunderstandings that often arise in conversations come from the lack of understanding of those two words: karma and justice.

In our Christianized culture, we perceive justice as being 'punishment', the need for the perpetrator to be remorseful and the victim to forgive. This is all a perversion of true justice and is an imbalance of the power expressed upon the Tree of Life as the sphere of Chesed/mercy. Mercy is an emotional expression of power without a counter balance of practical learning through bitter experience and removal of power (Geburah). The Christian religion expresses the power of Tiphareth only through Chesed, so the pure solar power of Tiphareth has to naturally re-balance itself in humanity through raw expression of Geburah; the result is the vicious side of this religion. If it is not consciously engaged by humanity, then the scales of the universe will engage it instead. The result of that unfocused raw power flowing through humanity is the genocides, inquisitions, self-inflicted cruelty, oppression etc. This unbalanced religious expression has permeated every facet of our Western culture and it leads to spiritual immaturity, destruction and degeneration. The deeper esoteric wisdom of justice, although depicted in some form in every courthouse, the blindfold Goddess of Justice with the scales and the sword, is dismissed out of hand.

Justice is about power in and power out. The scales, like the Tree of Life, have to be kept balanced so that the practitioner can handle power safely without getting blown up. The deeper into magic or spirituality you go, the stronger the need for justice in your life. If you live completely within the physical realm, then the sword of justice is slow and diffuse. The more you reach through the inner worlds through magic or spirituality, the more focused, pronounced and densely powerful the sword of justice becomes. When you take on specific magical responsibilities as an adept, then the scales become very finely balanced and knowingly taking a false step will result in swift results. The lesson of the unfolding energy will be sharp and to the point. And it will not come in the form of punishment, but in the form of bitter understanding through experience.

Justice is not about morals, it is about responsibility: if you do something that you know damages, hurts or deprives someone, then your 'power-scales' are at a deficit. As a magician, when you interact with the inner worlds, you automatically engage the rule of magical justice, known as the rule of Ma'at in ancient Egypt. Universal consciousness will place things in your path to teach you why your actions were unbalanced, so that you learn from bitter experience. That is a lesson that is hard to forget.Once the learning is in place, the energetic scales must be rebalanced. This is achieved by putting you in a situation whereby you observe an energetic 'debit', and you are given an opportunity to put your own action or energy into that debit to turn it into a credit.

The deeper you go into inner magic, the more profound the effects of justice are. If you reach through the inner worlds in an unbalanced pursuit of power and you are not ready to handle such power, you will blow yourself up. Cause and effect... put hand in fire, hand get burned. This will manifest either as literally going mad from the power, or being shut down magically. If you are totally incapable of handling large amounts of power, or powerful contacts, then the inner safety switch is thrown and you are left in the dark. This is done by the deeper part of you and is for your own good: you literally blow a fuse and end up in the dark.

If you have the natural or trained potential to handle vast amounts of power/contact and you go after that power in an unbalanced way, then you will be treated to a very hard lesson. The two possibilities are going mad or dying. Because you potentially have the ability to hold power, the inner fuse does not flip and the power flows into an unbalanced vessel and tips it over. It's all about personal responsibility, cause and effect; it's not about punishment.

This has been one of the biggest misunderstandings regarding the role of karma. Some people perceive the laws of karma to be based around an idea that your life is pre ordained, nothing can be changed and any shit in life you get is because you were bad in another life. That is not true and is a total misunderstanding of the law of karma. The law of karma is the same as the law of Ma'at or justice: everything is to be kept in balance or chaos occurs. The law of karma is the law of responsibility and understanding the natural consequences of actions.

So in magical practice, if you curse or attack someone, you are put into a dance of rebalancing the scales with them. If you magically interfere with nature for conditional human ends, then the results of that action will be set in motion and there is nothing that you can do to stop it. Once you realize that your simple thoughtless action is spreading out and causing untold damage, you cannot say sorry and stop it. You will have to observe the long unfolding of that action. And because your energy went into the initial action, your energy will be drawn upon throughout the unfolding of the action until it has run its course. This connection of energy to an action is that part that most people do not understand. This connection of energy will manifest in many ways, and the more profound the magical action, the more energy it will draw from you until it has fully run its course. With so much of your energy going in a justice direction, it will leave you energetically in deficit. This will manifest as inner weakness that will make you vulnerable to an endless list of imbalances, both energetic and magical.

If you try to compensate for such imbalance by using magic to draw more energy to you, or to enlist the help of beings, or to counteract the imbalance, then the imbalance will get longer and more pronounced as you draw more and more beings and power to your unbalanced orbit. The best advice is either; hunker down, accept the results of the energetic deficit and learn a hard lesson, or you can consciously engage the unfolding alone and offer yourself unconditionally in service to help re balance the scales. Working unconditionally, without specific intent or agenda, allows the energy to flow where it needs to and puts you in situations that will truly give you an opportunity to rebalance things. Often we can make things much worse by actions that we think will bring about rebalance but actually do not. This is because our understanding is often short sighted, and working blind with justice will side step such lack of understanding. This is why the statue of Justice is blindfolded: humanity cannot often perceive the whole picture and we need to work blind, unconditionally, trusting the flow of universal power to guide our hand. We surrender to the tide of universal power and yet keep our awareness focused so that we can learn from the events that manifest. That way, you will rebalance your scales and learn some good lessons.

4

Inner Contacts and Inner Beings

Studying and practicing magic will at some point or other, depending on which system of magic you are working with, bring you into direct contact with inner beings, i.e. beings/consciousness that are not a part of you (or your granny or the cat). These beings are part of the holism that is creation and jus because you cannot see them with your eyes does not mean they are not there. The magical interaction with these beings usually takes the form of visionary work, ritual invocation, or both.

Practicing magic will bring you into contact with all sorts of inner beings over the years and some of them will work with you in long term working partnerships. The most common working contact tends to be human, i.e. either they are dead and have chosen to stay in the inner worlds as a contact for humanity, or they are living contacts in their own time and place, working in the inner worlds as a contact. Sometimes there are human inner contacts that were part of a lodge, temple or order while in life, and after death they carry on their work with their order, acting as a go between or bridge between the inner and outer worlds. In the early stages of working with inner contacts, these are usually the type of inner contact or priest/ess that is brought through. They are worked with the most in earlier stages of magical work because their agendas, magical lines etc are well-known and usually fairly transparent.

Then there are contacts that are ancestors, land beings, deities, elemental beings and animals. Some of the ancestral contacts are very ancient beings from before our form of humanity. There are ancient beings that seem to be part human and part something else. Whatever the contact is, it is important not to get sidetracked by wanting to know who/what/where there are; you are brought together to do a job, not satisfy your curiosity or aid in agendas and theories.

There are inner contacts that are deep ancient combinations of human, deity and land power. These contacts are usually tied to a specific area and mediate the power of a particular force like a volcano, a fault line, a lake, a temple or a mountain etc. They probably started out as a human who worked intensively with land and faery beings connected to the site. Upon their death, the local magical shaman/ witch will have continued to work with the local faery or land being, and they will have merged with the human as they work from the realm of death. Slowly over the years the working union creates a merged form, which then presents as a deity. These contacts are powerful to work with but they still contain the frailty of the human spirit with all its inherent issues and hang-ups. That is why it is wise to tread carefully with a contact that presents as an ancient local deity, as most often they are composite beings.

Because of the spiritual propaganda of the monotheistic religions, almost all inner beings are considered evil and dangerous. Then you have the modern psychological 'slant', which states that these beings are all parts of us. These two primitive stances not only serve to separate us from interacting with these powerful beings, but they also create a deep imbalance that affects all of humanity. All beings have a purpose and are intimately interconnected: when we actively participate in this orchestra, harmony rules.

Some beings create life, and sustain power; others kill, damage or cull life forms. The need for light/dark, life/death, health/disease is paramount to the harmonic balance of the universe. When we step away from our role within that orchestra, like all other parts of nature, it quickly flies out of balance and the universe creates a counter balance in an attempt to rebalance the scales of existence. We see this response all around us, everyday. The more we cling to life at any cost and insist on over populating, over consuming and over building, the more nature and the balance of power responds with destruction.

There is also a level of inner contact that is human, or human in origin and survived the monotheistic 'slash and burn' conditioning as Saints. People in church ask them to intercede on their behalf and yet do not think of them as inner contacts or feel that they can just chat to them, ask them questions etc. Only in deepest darkest Catholicism will you still find people chatting and offering part of their meal to a 'Saint'. This is a form of working with an inner contact, just in the most difficult and unproductive way. In reality, human inner contacts span a whole complex weave of contact that is as fascinating as it is useful.

Human Inner Contact: dead or alive?

There are a variety of forms of inner contact that are or once were human. The first we will look at is the contact that was once human. Often these people were priests or priestesses, they were probably teachers but what they all have in common is that they were and are adepts in the greater mysteries. When an adept (and I mean a real adept, not a weekend course and paid a lot of money adept) dies, their knowledge of the death passage and experience of working in death while alive, allows them to make informed choices regarding whether to reincarnate or stay in the inner worlds to work as an inner contact. If they choose to stay out of the life circle and act in service as an inner contact, they will pass into a level of consciousness that is on the same 'frequency' for want of a better word, as the inner temples and inner library. Those magical workers in life who have connection to them, or people who are working on that same frequency will be able to find them and work with them both in vision and ritual.

If a beginner wishes to reach an inner adept as an inner contact, then they would need to be walking a similar magical path or one that has cross connections so that the same language is used. So for example if you wanted to reach W E Butler, or Dion Fortune, then working in the Western Mysteries in some form would give you the right frequency and vocabulary for productive communication. Reaching for such a contact is best attempted through a visionary visit to the inner library. That is if they want to work with you, sometimes they may just tell you to piss off. But if you were studying Vodun, Siberian Magic, or Indonesian Magic, then trying to reach such Western contacts through such non-Western systems is unlikely to work.

If you ask unconditionally for help, then the teacher who is best equipped to help you will come to your aide. Some of the famous adepts were brilliant magicians, but many also had their baggage. And there are the ones who were great writers and communicators, but magically left a lot to be desired. Some adepts became famous just by virtue of their ability to sound like they knew what they were talking about, and some just because they had money and were able to get their work in print. So do not try and reach for a 'name', just ask for help.

Living contacts

Contacts that are alive and in their own time are the most fascinating to work with. How this works is as follows – an adept works through vision and ritual, offering themselves in service as a contact to assist in particular magical tasks that are relevant to them. They work through the inner worlds in vision, usually while also working in ritual, appearing in the inner or outer magical space/temple as an inner contact. They can be from the same time as you, or from your past or future. It is a fascinating and little understood area of contact magic.

When you work with living inner contacts, there are certain things that you need to bear in mind when approaching such a contact. Firstly, do not assume that because he or she is a magical adept that they will be all knowing, all wise and all ethical. Nothing could be further from the truth. Some of the most screwed up people I know are also gifted magical adepts. When you are working with a living adept, you have to be aware that because their consciousness is rooted in a living body somewhere, their spirit will be subject to all the emotional baggage that the chemical soup of neurotransmitters inflicts. So if that adept has mental/emotional problems, then you will be on the receiving end of whatever instability they express in daily life.

You will also be exposed to any inner parasites or worse that are hitching a ride on the adept. If that adept has a magical tie or oath binding upon them and their communication with you breaks that oath, then you will be subject to any whiplash from that oath breaking. So you can see that working with living inner contacts can be fascinating, but also riddled with dangers and potholes. In these circumstances, a very good eye for bullshit, lies and unhealthy spirits is paramount if you are to do such work.

If you do not wish to have your call answered by a living adept, then you can plainly say so in your call through the worlds. As an aside, it would be wise to use similar common sense when you are looking for a teacher in your own time, in the flesh. Again, just because a magician is brilliant doesn't mean that they are also mentally balanced. And just because an adept says that they are a good person doesn't really mean that they are, it just means that they could be a good liar. Again, it is all down to the bullshit meter, also known as discernment. That meter works well when you are not desperate for something. If you have a desperate longing for magical learning, then call out that desperation while in the inner library, which is a safe structure designed to filter out unhealthy people. Life doesn't have those filters; you have to provide them for yourself.

I have worked as an inner contact in rituals both in real time, in the past and the future. Physically it can be very draining, but it does expand our understanding of inner contacts when this form of work is done. It will be discussed in detail in book III of this series, which is based around adept magical techniques.

Abyss, Humanity and Souls

The inner structure, fate of the species and death/birth flow of humanity passes through the inner landscape known as the Desert and the Abyss. This inner landscape is expressed in Kabbalah as the Tree of Life, but as an inner landscape it appears as a desert with the Abyss separating universal power/divinity from the physical outer manifestation of universal power, which is basically all of creation. For us as humans, that outer manifestation of universal power is humanity.

When humans make love, the frequencies of energy stretch through the inner worlds in search of consciousness. The power of that energy is specifically for bridging a consciousness from A to B. That bridging power can be used to either access a place or to mediate a being depending upon the focus and intent of those making love. If there is no intent other than pleasure or breeding, then the energy gravitates towards a being.

What being comes through into the vessel (womb) depends upon the balance and clarity of the lovemaking, and of the people involved. Now such a statement can quickly bring about a moral kneejerk reaction, which is not necessary. This is not a moral issue, but an energetic issue. The emotion and imagination used in the lovemaking is the key. If the emotion is violent, sadistic or unbalanced, that is the energetic frequency that will be put out as a beacon for a new life. The same goes for the use of the imagination. Imagination is the key doorway in magic between all the worlds, so what a magician does with their imagination is of paramount importance. The focused use of imagination in lovemaking is the filter through which a being can flow. If that imagination is used in a violent, unhealthy or corrupt way, then such a filter will only allow beings/souls of that pattern to come through. If such a sex act is conducted within a framework of magical power then the frequency will reach much further into the Abyss and will pull out powerful destructive beings.

If the couple is sterile/doesn't have a womb or is using contraceptives, then the being will still come through, it just will not manifest into physical form. A skilled magician/priestess however can bridge that mediated being into a physical form i.e. a statue etc. They need to know how to get it back out if it goes feral, and most importantly, what it actually is that you are bridging into our world. Once here, beings are really hard to get rid of if they create chaos.

The same is true for lovemaking that is focused towards a spiritual intent, where a magical couple involve themselves in ritual sex to bring through a 'higher' being, king or priest/ess. The use of energy and focused imagination is applied during the sex act to reach up the Abyss to the powers of divinity, angelic consciousness etc. Such ritual sex can bring through either a physical being or an inner being into this world.

Now if these acts are viewed as 'bad' or 'good', then the two camps continuously bring imbalance into our world. If some group brings into being a 'higher consciousness' that would have not naturally manifested in our world but was brought in by magic/ritual, then the outer world immediately becomes imbalanced. To counter that balance a being from deeper down the Abyss must be brought into the world. If this is not actively done, nature will do it for us, in a far harsher and abrupt way. This is the root of the problem with the whole messiah concept. Judaism is littered with stories of angels and demons called into the world by temple priests or prophets that in turn leads to an energetic need for a counter balance.

This creates a cascading situation whereby humanity causes a mess, then uses sacred magic to bring through a messiah to save us from our own mess, nature responds by sending a chaotic or destructive being to counter it. Thus you have a dance of the devil and the messiah that we see in Abrahamic religions. The same happens at different levels, different octaves of the same action/reaction. If you purposely reach for a pure messiah to manifest, the balance of power will counter by bringing forth destructive beings. Hence Christianity with its lessons of love, passivity and compassion, in practice manifests war, torture, mass murderers and perversions.

This imbalance is not only caused by ritual sex but by humanity's actions in general. This can express itself in any manner of ways when humanity is out of touch with the powers of creation. A tiny example but one that is so visible today is the flood of population. We have embroiled ourselves in a battle of wills with nature, and due to the unbalanced stance of the monotheistic religions, this battle is pushing us close to the edge of the Abyss.

The roles of destroying deities and demonic powers

In times past, cultures worked closely with destroying deities and demonic powers along with creative deities and other beings. A very good example of such harmonic balance was the Egyptian concept of 'Maat,' which was both a deity and a method of operating as humans in the world. Destroying deities were respected and worked with to keep the balance, and their actions were respected and accepted. Humanity attempted to live with and adjust to such destroying principles, until it realized it could manipulate, bind and clash with such powers to its own advantage. The transition from respecting power to attempting to harness and control power was a degenerate step for humanity and has consequently led to the mess we are in. These destructive beings bring disease, war, death and natural disasters that keep living beings in check. So how as magicians can we work with such powers?

The first step is to understand these powers, their functions in our world and our own responsibility. The outer manifestation of a destroying deity and demonic powers are personalities, a human constructed interface that we used first to communicate with and then control the deity/being. Over the generations, as human power agendas changed, so did our explanations of the mythology, image and function of the deity. So for example a Near Eastern female destroying power of the desert and bringer of disease was transformed, by religious spin, into a sexual predatory vamp that ate babies and turned men mad. The more people formed that image in their minds, the stronger that construct became until a parasitical being was more than happy to step into the role, thus it becomes a 'reality'. The original power still raged in the form of desert storms, and disease. So a battle ensues between humanity, natural disasters and illnesses. Instead of respecting the destroying power of nature, we build in its path so the storm/ earthquake/flood etc wreaks havoc with our population. It is much better to not build, but to commune with the inner power behind the natural manifestation and learn to respect it. Tuning into natural power helps us build a relationship with it so that we get advanced warning of oncoming potential disasters.

Similarly respecting the need to keep the population in balance, the need for nature to inflict death and disease lessens. With fewer babies, there are more resources and better communal parenting. There are still examples of this happening in 'stone age' cultures scattered around the world, (Andaman Islands, Amazon etc) although they are almost extinct from civilization encroaching upon the resources. Nature does intervene where she can though. When a population is getting out of control, female babies abort more often and the population generally gets more aggressive. When there is a threat to the population, i.e. natural disasters or major stresses, all but the strongest male babies abort whereas more female babies survive. This ensures a better chance

88

of species survival (culled cohort theory-Dr Ralph Catalano, professor of public health at the University of California, Berkeley)

What we can do

The first and probably most important step would be to develop a working practice whereby the magician works with beings in their own place and time rather than dragging them into our world. The second would be to work consciously, in cooperation with the beings and powers that do express themselves through our world. This can be done by working with weather powers (as opposed to controlling and manipulating them) and building respectful relationships with them. By working this way, you slowly begin to understand the inner dynamics of these powers and the effects that they have on human consciousness stretching far beyond simple weather patterns. The same can be said of land powers, beings of this world and deities. By stepping back and looking at what these powers actually bring to the world, and looking beyond our own needs and wants, we begin to see an intricate dance of consciousness and power that constantly keeps the land and all living beings in balance. That does not mean that these beings will favor our survival, rather we will begin to understand that death and destruction is all a part of the health of the land and all species.

Accepting that a storm, weather pattern, or disease outbreak is doing a needed job, and learning how to operate with that power rather than clash with it, changes how we view our roles as humans. By changing how we perceive those roles, we change the impact upon us, rolling with the punches and learning. Taking an active role in assisting the power can change the way we view such disasters. It doesn't stop them, but they become a bigger part of us. The nearer towards a healthy balance we move, the less likely such expressions of power will devastate us.

One way of taking an active role in balance with the land is to first come to know the land upon which you live in intimate detail. Walking the land, visiting the water, the hills, learning where the weather patterns come from and go to, tuning into fault lines and the seasons, all of these actions benefit the land upon which you live, and helps to enter into a working relationship with the land and its inherent beings. If you live on land that has ancient burials, it will teach you about where the places of death and life are. Visiting the burials and talking with them, honoring the places of death and giving gifts of food to the places of life are all simple acts that help to build a relationship with the land. Once that communion is established, then communing with the storms, the Sun, the Moon, the caves, the rivers and the trees all connect us to the larger tides of consciousness that flow through the land.

The next step beyond the passive communion is the active listening through instinct, inner contacts and body reactions. Through listening we begin to build an active conversation with the powers around us, which enable us to have deeper magical relationships with the immensely powerful beings that manifest through the landscape. Our imagination builds an interface of characters that enable us to understand these powers in a more human way and as long as we do not try to control them, a working relationship can build where the storms, seas, rivers etc communicate their tides of power and alert us to any imbalance. Through that relationship we can begin to learn what the role is that we need to take up in our dance with these forces.

What becomes a human/animal type interface is usually an intermediary being that becomes the voice of the power and acts an interpreter between humanity and the nature force. That intermediary will step into the interface we have created, and if there is specific focused magical intent to create such an interface for a mediator, then any opportunist and potentially rogue beings will be filtered out. The more established the intermediary becomes, the more it fuses with the nature power so that it become intertwined with the nature force. So when we commune with the goddess of the river, the interface translates needs and actions between humanity and nature. Some of the more ancient nature deities are still active and do respond to human interaction. They will, if a relationship is built with them, warn of coming fluctuations of their power, (i.e. storms, floods), communicate their needs for honoring and will be keen to express outrage at human actions that cause imbalances.

By working closely with these beings, we can build up a better understanding of the tides and flows of the powers within the land around us, which in turn can educate us as to how to live alongside these powers properly, rather than harnessing, controlling and manipulating them. They will show us how to act to trigger rebalance as unconditional catalysts, and warn us as to the difficulties that will be experienced for us in that rebalance process.

Thought forms and passive enlivening

There are areas of magic where it is considered part and parcel of the art to create and develop thought forms. These are used for a number of tasks, including guarding, attacking, watching etc. Thought forms are beings created straight from the imagination of the magician and powered by his own energy to fulfill his or her agenda. Such practice takes a lot of mental discipline to ensure that the thought form stays under control. Thought forms can go feral very easily and their antics are fed by the magician's own energy which can result in a major energy deficit. The stability of the thought form is only as good as the mental focus and stability of its creator, as it is basically an extension and projection of their imagination.

The major problem that can arise from the use of thought forms, when created in a lodge setting, is the question of energy *source*. Unscrupulous lodge/group leaders can engage the group in the creation of a thought form or inner temple, and use the energy of the group to power such creations. It's a form of scape-goating. The group's energy creates and feeds the thought forms, and also takes the consequences of what the thought form does. So if it goes feral and does damage, kills etc, it is the group who carry the energetic burden, not the leader. This is sadly a common practice of some larger, more public lodges that have a huge membership that involves initiation. The small inner group creates the form and the rest of the membership take the hit for what goes wrong.

Personally I think thought forms are more trouble than they are worth, and it is much better and safer for magical projects and jobs to work with real inner beings (as opposed to created ones). Creating thought forms can very easily lead to digging very deep holes for oneself that take a lot of energy and effort to deal with. The other issue with thought forms, particularly if they are used to attack someone, is that their combat power is only as strong as the mental focus and life force of the person who created and is powering them. If the victim happens to be stronger, then the attacker is liable not only to have wasted a lot of energy for nothing (ever spent a bored afternoon swatting feeble thought forms sent from a disgruntled lodge? Great fun), but the person or group can potentially put their egregore at risk. If the thought form is connected to the egregore as an energy source, then a skilled victim can not only dismantle the thought form, but track the umbilical back to the egregore and then dismantle the egregore itself. So all in all, I really think they are a total waste of time.

Golems

A step up the skill ladder is the making of a Golem. Contrary to popular belief, Golems are not manifest beings that we can see with the eye, they are inner beings created out of the element of earth and enlivened with the sacred breath and the word of power, usually written on the forehead but sometimes in a hidden place on the clay body. The power of consciousness is in the clay body, but it is the 'inner' body of the Golem that then goes out to do its master's bidding. So it is a soulless being that is a slave to its creator.

Destroying a Golem is fairly straightforward, but it must be done correctly. Finding that actual clay body and erasing the word of power from it will not destroy the Golem, it will only destroy the being's link to the physical realm, and will also free it from its bind to its maker. To be rid of the Golem, the word of power must be located on its inner body and wiped out at that level. To wipe off the Aleph from the word Emet leaves Met, which is death and as such destroys the Golem. It is ritually sent back into the earth from whence it came and if possible the clay figure is similarly destroyed.

The making of a Golem takes a great deal of energy, as it uses your essence to operate: you breathe life into it and it works from your 'sacred breath'. Golems are not usually put to good use, are dangerous and are akin to putting an AK-47 into the hands of an immature short-tempered idiot with an axe to grind.

It is good to remember that in truth, you never get away with a silly or vicious act: there is no punishment or judgement, true, but there is usually a massive energetic payback at some point and I have watched such things with people over and over. If you really have to have a go at someone, just bloody well punch them and have done with it!

Passive enlivening

Passive enlivening is a very interesting phenomenon that I have had some interesting results with, and I have also seen some epic disasters. There are two main forms of passive enlivening, intentional and unintentional. Let's take the unintentional first as that one can create the most spectacular booboos.

Unintentional passive enlivening is the accidental creation of a door in an object or image that a being steps into and begins to interact with the humans around it. What causes this unintentional door/ threshold to appear is either the natural ability of a human or thoughtless action by a trained magician. If for example you are a highly trained magician who is used to working in the inner worlds and conversing with many different types of beings, then the ability within you to mediate, call and access different worlds and beings is probably very strong. So if, for example, you mindlessly begin to chat with, say, an ornamental statue of a deity, being or person, there will come a point when said statue or image will begin to chat back. The process from behind the scenes goes a little like this: Magician gets bored and talks to statue, the fact that the magician is programmed from an inner sense to reach through worlds means that whenever there is conversation, ears prick up, thresholds are created, doors are opened - what ever you do with your imagination as a magician has magical potential. So, because it is unfocussed, there is a good chance that a passing parasite or faery being with a warped sense of humor picks up on the communion potential and steps into the statue to use it as an interface.

The other possibility is that the magician unconsciously creates a thought form that resides in the image or statue, which again has the potential to go feral or become the vessel for passing beings looking for an interaction meal. The deeper the magician works in the inner worlds and communes with inner world beings, the more potential there is for such things to happen. It has happened to me a few times... I talk to things all the time. Sometimes when you get someone who has natural ability or was magically adept in another life and is not aware of it in this life, beings will walk into statues and images in attempts to connect or build parasitical relationships. I have observed this in children who have natural ability - their teddy is a wee bit more than the shop advert claimed... The long and short of it is; if you are going to talk to inanimate objects, make sure it is intentional and that you are ready for a being coming through and talking back.

Intentional passive enlivening is an interesting magical technique that involved picking or making a statue or image and beginning to treat it as though it is a real being as opposed to an object. With focused intent, the right form of communion and repetitive interactions, the being you are reaching for will commune with you through the object, or a being that will mediate between you and the target being will use the object as a window. This is a different method from ritual enlivenment or magical entrapment but can be just as effective.

The mechanism is simple. The statue or image is an image of a known being/god/goddess and you talk to the image as if you were talking directly to that being on a daily basis. Because of the focused intent, the repetitive action and the relative conversation, all done by a person with inner connections, pathways of inner communication on specific magical frequencies begin to open. They strengthen with each day of communion and usually first attract a type of mediator being who acts as a preparer and go between for the communion. As the contact becomes established, the deity/being that the image represents begins to commune and interact through the image. Hence the enlivenment is complete.

So what can go wrong? Oh hell, loads of things. The mishaps can range from feral thought forms, to hungry parasites to aggressive/territorial beings to demanding deities that refuse to go, and wish for your attention and homage day in and day out. Sometimes these deities have a limited shelf life in that they will commune with you for a while and will then pack up and go when they have achieved what they wanted, or they think you are an idiot, or both. Because it is all done passively, i.e. as part of everyday life, the whole situation can be harder to deal with as they embed themselves into your living environment.

On the other hand you can passively enliven objects/images to bring through uardian beings that will watch your home and warn you of inner intrusion, power build ups and other odd happenings. They may wish for something in return - I had a wonderful hardworking guardian being who loved shiny things, for example.

It is also a technique used within the Catholic Church, as opposed to ritual enlivenment. The statue of the Saint is prayed to constantly and over a period of time a being connected to that consciousness steps into the image and begins to interact or intercede. The blessing of the object, and the 'dedication' ensure that a specific line of communication opens slowly as opposed to random beings stepping in. It's not as effective or powerful as the earlier Egyptian ritual methods of bringing through deities into statues. That technique was far more powerful and enduring. The essential difference between the two methods is that passive enlivening needs near constant communication for the bridge to stay open. Once the communion stops on the part of the human, the inner contact dies away.

With specific ritual enlivenment it is totally different. Ritually, a fragment of the consciousness of the deity is brought into substance and stays there wherever that substance exists. It is the root of the concept of transubstantiation in Catholicism. (Christian rituals, particularly from the Roman Empire, i.e. Catholic, are fragments of earlier Pagan rituals) Therefore an ancient statue of say, Sekhmet, is very likely to retain echoes of her power. If the magician, who is adept at inner communication, visits a museum, he is very likely to pick up on the calls and demands of those deities as they try to communicate through the images. It is important to note that the power is within the original statue that was ritually enlivened, not the generic image. So a copy of the image will be just an image and nothing more.

It is good to remember this when you buy or obtain an ancient relic that is ritually enlivened: it is not an ornament or magical plaything; it is real, potentially powerful, demanding and possibly dangerous. When you get bored of playing with that deity and want to partake of the New Age shopping frenzy for gods and goddesses, be aware that the being that is bridging through the image or statue may not have finished with you and will not be prepared to let go until it is ready. There is a whole major can of worms that can be opened with such behavior.

The single most important thing to remember when you create a thoughtform, a window for a being etc, is that the action is caused solely by you. Any chaos, destruction, major change in fate, anything that upsets the balance of order is your responsibility alone. That doesn't mean you can say sorry, or that you can stick a finger up at the universe...well, if you do it will be ignored, it means that energetically you are responsible to set the balance right. People assume, mainly because of the religions of today, that 'God' is a conscious being who is like a parent, that God will smile indulgently at his naughty creations and let them off with a smack. That is not correct and it never ceases to amaze me that people think that way. Divinity is power, universal power that flows through everything and enlivens or destroys. It has no emotion. It operates through a rule of balance within an imbalanced world, and beings operate within that world to constantly keep the plates spinning. Fate is tied up with this path of constant striving for balance, and what we call karma is the dynamic that operates through life to balance the scales. In real terms, the very powerful beings i.e. archangelic beings, are aware of balance and imbalance and they are driven to action from that standpoint. It has nothing to do with emotion.

Beings that have physical form have emotions, as do inner beings that once had physical form or an inner projection of form. This makes it easier for us to interact with this type of being than the major angelic powers and beyond, where emotion is not their greatest quality. So beings that are close to us, who help or hinder us, can come across as nurturing or destroying. We respond to this output of emotive interchange by building relationships or interactions with these beings, and one of the lessons to be recovered from such interaction is the understanding that we basically haven't a clue what we are doing and every time we act, we usually mess it up.

So if you create a thought form or enliven an object that causes destruction where destruction was not needed, that creates an energy deficit that you have to fill. You would carry the burden of that deficit and the energy would leak from your life, or your belongings, or anything else that can fill that void. The twists and weaves of these energy dances are awesome in their complexity. If however that deficit was needed, your actions have fulfilled it through your magical work. Because of this complex dynamic, one can become paranoid about every action, which is not a productive way forward. A better possible way to approach it is either to work unconditionally with inner contacts or to double check your work first.

Working unconditionally with inner contacts is a method of work that you can come to once you have built up a good working relationship with inner contacts that you trust. You agree to work unconditionally for what is needful, and they put things in your path that need to be dealt with magically. So for example with enlivening an object, you will have a perceived magical need that has to be attended to, or they will have a job for you. An object or image will be placed in your path for you to work with and you would mediate whatever is necessary from the inner worlds into the object. So you can see how trust is a major thing with this method and you really have to know that your inner contact is solid and legitimate.

Double checking work before you commence is another method of dodging the scales chaos. If you need to bring something through or create something, obviously it has to be for a purpose – doing this type of magic just because you can is the path of the immature idiot. Anyhow, once you have decided that it really needs doing, it is time to check the outcomes, short and long term, of such actions. The way to do this is through Tarot or your own designed deck, which is usually more specific and accurate. That way, you cannot kid yourself that such work needs doing. You must always look at the long-term consequences as well as the short-term immediate problem outcome, as magic can ripple for generations and cause chaos in the future.

I use both methods, unconditional and double-checking. There have been many times that I was convinced a certain action was needed, but then when I checked it, the outcome long term was very bad for all concerned, so I didn't do it. The solution often plopped down in front of me when I wasn't expecting it. This is the other interesting thing about working deeply in magic and the inner worlds: the beings that keep the balance of power in and out begin to work closely with you. If you are consecrated, then fate can sometimes really speed up and these guys are constantly around you guiding you this way and that in your work to ensure you do what needs to be done. They often block you from work when it is imbalanced and basically nanny you through certain situations. This is not because they care about you; they are ensuring that the flow of energy is going where it needs to.

Similarly, if you go too deeply into the inner realms and get too close to the threshold of divinity, the major beings that keep the world in balance, the Archon and the Aeon, will knock you back and probably blow your body fuse so that you cannot do that again. Their job is to keep humanity and the power of Divinity apart so that humanity cannot grab that power.

Part Two -
The work of the Lone
Practitioner

The work of the lone practitioner is a very hard but extremely rewarding one that really and truly puts you on the path of powerful magic. Nothing is done for you, you are not babysat through your training, and your path of work is something that comes from your choice alone, not the dictates of a group. It also allows a magician to forge his or her own path in a direction that is perfect for them.

In truth, the life of a magician tends to be a mixture of group and lone practice. Sometimes groups are put in our path for a length of time for us to learn something, and other times groups and teachers evade us so we are thrown back on our own resources and initiative. Magic, like life does not start and end in a group – we are born alone, and we die alone. We walk the path through life and magic with people around us, sometimes very close to us, but ultimately our development and practice is within ourselves.

The first and last rule of magical development, for both beginner and experienced practitioner is discernment. That word should be tattooed on everyone's forehead so that it is the first thing you read each morning when you look in the mirror. As we grow into adulthood and maturity, we learn how to spot the con artist, the possible dangers in life, the good things, the bad things and the just plain stupid. We learn not to talk to strangers, not to stick our fingers in electrical sockets or touch live wires, we learn to be careful near cliffs, near bears, and not to poke rattlesnakes. So why the hell don't we carry that lesson of maturity into magic?

Some people approach magic with all the wisdom and foresight of a curious three year old. And as a result of that quaint naivety, they end up drained, depressed and parasitized. On the other hand if you approach magic with extreme cynicism and over caution, you will never get anywhere. There needs to be a balance between caution, curiosity, an open and exploratory mind, and a good inner alarm system. A good bullshit meter will also shave years off of your search for learning. There is a tremendous amount of bullshit out there and keeping an awareness of that fact will be very helpful.

1

Visionary magic

Visionary magic is the use of the imagination to structure a door whereby the magician can pass into the inner realms or astral realm. It is an ancient form of magical practice, though I was surprised to read an academic article the other day, which claimed it was new. Nothing could be further from the truth. The use of structured vision combined with ritual, as opposed to spontaneous vision, is one of the most powerful and ancient ways to conduct magic. The methods were usually passed from teacher to student, as the easiest way to gain this skill is through resonance, and the keys to the visionary paths were written into many ancient texts. And this is one of the greatest joys when treading a magical path as a student: coming upon an ancient text or painting and seeing/reading the keys of the vision before you; you recognize them instantly, not because you studied them, but because you had direct experience.

Without visionary techniques to access the inner realms, or (astral realms as some people call them), magic gets stuck on the ground like a plane without an engine. The power that fuels ritual comes from inner flexibility that in turn comes from visionary work conducted regularly over a period of time. Meditation prepares the mind for visionary work by teaching the student how to still their minds and focus. From that focused point the student learns first how to access thresholds within themselves and later, thresholds to the inner worlds.

Meditation can take a very simple form, and the simpler the better. Learning to breathe calmly and freely without force is the first step. Sitting still, be aware of the breath as it regulates its own rhythm. Once that is achieved, then counting the out breath up to ten and then going back to one and starting again is the next step. If the mind wanders even slightly during the counting, then the student should start back at one and count the breaths up to ten again. From there, seeing the in breath as white smoke and breathing out black smoke while counting focuses the mind further into a specific action. Again, if the mind becomes distracted, go back to one and start over again. This simple breathing exercise should be done morning and night until it can be performed without distraction, wandering of the mind or shifting of the body. One does not have to assume difficult or odd poses, but the back must be supported to ensure clear breathing.

When the student has become accustomed to the breathing exercise then it is time to turn the mind inwards to the inner centre or threshold of the void. This can be focused upon as an inner flame, which burns quietly within your centre. After starting the meditation with the breathing exercise, see a flame burning quietly and calmly within. Just hold the focus of the flame with no other thought and sit silently in the presence. Once that image has been established, see water beneath the flame, held naturally as if by a membrane that has no description other than it holds water. Once the combination of inner flame and water can be held in meditation without distraction then it is time to make the step from meditation to vision.

The first step of visionary work.

Visionary work can quickly be taken up by the mind as a browsing pastime, which must be avoided at all costs. This discipline has become much harder for young people who have been exposed to years of video games: the mind expects to be playing, changing focus etc. The focus of meditation trains the mind away from such distractions and allows the natural visionary skills of the human to surface.

To begin with the student needs to learn how to access the deepest and yet simplest mystery within visionary magic and that is the void from which all flows into the worlds and to which all flows back. It is the beginning and end of all magic and cannot be reiterated enough. It is within us and everything around us: it is the threshold of existence. It is represented within the Tarot as the Fool card, which begins the major arcana and also ends the major arcana.

To access the void, record the following vision on to a tape or ipod so that you can listen. This external voice will guide you until you are sure of what you are doing and where you are going. Once you have become used to this meditation and know what you are doing, stop using the recording and work naturally. This method of initially using a recording is a good way forward in most new visionary work if you do not have someone there to guide you who knows what they are doing.

Vision of the Void

See the flame over water within you and be with it quietly until your mind is still. Once you are in full stillness, see the flame grow bigger until it is all around you. Standing up in the flame, with the water flowing beneath it, you feel the gentle cool power of the flame of life flow through you. The flame does not burn you, but refreshes you, and your spirit recognizes the feeling deep within. From that still place, see yourself stepping out of the flame into nothing. You step through the fire threshold to find yourself in a place that has no time, no movement, no image: it is truly nothing that is full of potential.

In that place, you realize you have no boundaries, no body and no earth life: this is the threshold of the eternal soul. Feel yourself spreading out in the nothing, drifting and expanding in stillness and silence. In that place, you feel the power of all being flow within and all around you. Do not let your mind wander into thought patterns, just bathe in the stillness until you are ready to come out. When you are ready, be aware of your earthly life and human form. Feel yourself come back into an image of your earthly body and when that is complete, see the flame as a wall of fire before you. Step into the flame, bathing in its energy while being aware of the water beneath it which flows through you, sustaining you. Slowly bring your consciousness back to the fact that the flame sits deep within you, in the centre of your body. Be aware of yourself sitting quietly, with the flame and water in your centre. Be aware of your breathing, be aware of your surroundings and when you are ready, open your eyes.

* * *

This vision of the void should be worked with every day until it becomes second nature. It is the most powerful vision and yet the most simple that you will ever use. Over time, you will learn how to access this place in an instance, just by the thought, which will instantly put you in a deep and still place. If you are ever in a dangerous inner situation (like having a demonic titan being rushing towards you with teeth bared) it can instantly put you in a place and state where very little can touch you or get a hold of you. If you are in the total stillness of the void, there is nothing for an inner being to grab: you have no boundaries, no form and your consciousness is suddenly out of their frequency. It must be practiced regularly throughout your magical life and never forgotten or cast to one side. It has saved my life on more than one occasion.

When the student is able to go in and out of the void with no distraction and with ease, then it is time to practice such meditation/ vision while walking with the eyes open. After a few years of practice, you can walk down a busy high street full of noise and distraction and yet be still within the void as you walk. You will affect the energy of everything around you by mediating the stillness and silence, calming down chaotic energies as you pass by.

The void vision, along with the breath meditation prepares the mind and soul for the hard work of visionary magic and it truly is very hard work, both physically and spiritually. Moving power around at great depths and heights needs a body and spirit that is strong, focused, disciplined and able to work under any circumstances. The simple void vision is the first step in that preparation.

The next step: discovery of the world

Before the student begins to delve into magical structures it is important to be aware of one's surroundings i.e. the inner manifestations of the land upon which we live. The inner landscape and the immediate realms surrounding that landscape are important foundations for any magical work. It is pointless reaching for the Moon if you do not know what is in one's own backyard. This can be accessed first through a series of simple but potentially profound visions and then worked with in basic ritual to ground, root and develop the magical mind.

It is also important for the student who begins the path of learning visionary magic to be aware of the necessity for inner and outer boundaries. These boundaries do not have to be in place forever, and indeed as each generation develops, the need for boundaries will change depending upon the consciousness of the student and the culture in which they live. These early boundaries are to safe guard the mind and spirit of the student: natural visionary students can be drawn into vision haphazardly to satisfy their curiosity or to push boundaries early on. This opens the student up to the dangers of parasites, feral beings and the latent imbalances within their own personality. Visionary work carries great power with it and as with all great powers, caution is an all repeating mantra.

Once the boundaries are in place, the student can begin to learn the inner highway code of conduct, the basics of 'stranger danger' and safely find the pathways to various realms without too many mishaps. In times past, magical lodges had very strict boundaries in place, and in many lodges those same boundaries are still in place, but the original purpose for them seems to have been forgotten. Those boundaries reflected the consciousness of the time and although we have moved on in the way we think and feel, such boundaries have not kept pace with the evolution of the spirit and mind. Some lodges still use a very slow and cumbersome ladder of inner contacts, along with strict grades, top heavy rituals and an abundance of rules, regulations and secrecy oaths. New contacts are rarely sought and the health/balance of the current contacts is rarely challenged. Instead, only the information given by the contacts is challenged and this is usually conducted through trance mediumship with the occasional foray into vision. Such a working pattern traps the flow of power into a small pot. The rigid reliance upon a small group of recent human inner contacts, communed with through a tight hierarchy, strangles the potential for deeper, older and more profound non human contacts. It also potentially blocks more ancient human contacts that can be worked with directly, rather than through a 'chain of command'.

If we truly want to move forward, then the initial boundaries need to keep pace with our minds and spirits, without losing the quality of the protection that boundaries can give. Magic is moving closer and closer in small steps towards recognition of the power of nature in a mature respectful manner as opposed to an older attitude of dominion and control. Nature can be utilized magically to create boundaries, which gives us a purer and more malleable form to work with.

What are boundaries?

In visionary magic, the 'boundaries' are the paradigm that you work in. The landscape, the contacts, the method for opening the contact, the method for closing the contact, all create a format to work within. If it is a format that has been used before, then it is a well-trodden path but can also be a corrupt, so discernment and common sense are good things to keep switched on. If the path is newly forged, then it is more important to take one's time over the vision, be mindful of building up the paths, structures and images carefully so that they strengthen. The dangers are if it is a new path and the person walking the path has little or no experience in visionary magic, then the ability to differentiate between real and imaginary, healthy and non healthy contacts is weak.

My personal belief is that if you work initially within frameworks that have been previously used, the student can hone their skills well before striking out alone. The boundaries, contacts, ground rules and power is already solid which allows the student to progress. It is important to remember that such a path is not the be all and end all, that eventually if the student wishes to truly work with depths of power and be of service they will need at some point to leave the structure behind.

Practical methods for foundation training

Once the ability to be still and meditate have been accomplished, and the void is accessed without the imagination drifting, then it is time to learn some foundation visions and rituals to train the mind and body in preparation for magical work. The following method/path is just one of many, but it is one I have personally trodden for a very long time so I am fully aware of its strengths and weaknesses. It is a series of methods and visions that stretch back in terms of usage for millennia, and many Western Mystery magicians will recognize fragments of this path.

The structure of the training in this path is geared towards training the practitioner to be able to access certain inner temples and inner contacts that have long term connections to both our own land and the mixed culture that we live in. Once work has been established with the contacts gained from these visions, then the practitioner will begin to get a deeper understanding of some of the other magical paths that are around us today – the deeper into the inner worlds you go, the less difference you will find between cultures, religions and magical paths.

When you work with these visions there are a few pointers that will be helpful to remember. Don't do visions lying down; it is too easy to drift off to sleep. Sit in a straight backed chair so that you stay conscious. Along with the obvious turn the phone off and lock the door, it is important to remember to have a focal point to work from, like a candle flame or bowl of water. Both are sacred elements and should be worked with respectfully. The other important point is the use of the imagination and learning how to discipline it. The general rule of thumb is; always treat what you see in vision as real, unless you start to get the Disney channel. Treating all imaginative interactions as real breaks down the barriers that our culture erects in us where we end up questioning everything. That shuts down the bridge of communion with the inner worlds very quickly. Once you have become used to working in vision, certain aspects of the vision will begin to solidify and you will start to recognize what is real and what is just your imagination. Eventually you will learn to filter your own imagination out naturally so that interactions are clear and powerful.

Another important rule to remember is, do not use the vision as entertainment and do not veer from the intended vision and vanish into flights of fancy. Too many people follow their curiosity or flights of fancy and end up losing their contact as they play in a pool of imagination.

It takes great discipline to develop the inner 'muscle' for true visionary magic. This is one of the places where a need for self-imposed boundaries comes in. Once that discipline is in place, then it is far easier to go on exploratory missions, as you will very easily be able to ascertain what is a real contact and what is not, and you will be able to access many inner realms without danger of letting your imagination take over.

Keeping a diary of your visions and experiences is very important so that you can go back and look in years to come. It also helps one to remember what happened, what contacts where made, and what your responses where. Later on, when you are reading about the subject matter and you come across something that you saw in vision, it will help to confirm your experiences. And this is another exciting part of visionary magic: you will see, hear and meet many different types of beings, and they will teach you or tell you things. Later, such information will manifest in the outside world, or something they predicted will happen. It is a wonderful feeling when you are first venturing into the inner worlds and you get absolute solid evidence for yourself that it is real and it works. Many years later, I still smile when that happens, which is often.

Practical visions and background information

Once the technique of inner visionary work has been established, then it is time to go through various realms to learn about them, make inner contacts/find inner teachers etc. The first place to venture to is the place closest to home, i.e. the inner landscape that is all around you. Getting to know the land upon which you live is a very important step towards grounding, service and also to learn your own place in the grand scheme of things. The vision of the inner land is an ancient mythical vision that takes us to the depths of the Northern Hemisphere. Wherever you are, this vision will link you deep into the ancient memory of the land. If you live in the Southern Hemisphere, you will have to experiment with this vision and see where it takes you. Record the following visions so that they guide you through the vision until you know your way there and back without help.

The Vision of the Inner Land

Light a candle, close your eyes and be still. With your inner vision, see a flame burning quietly within you, the flame that burns at the edge of the void. In vision, reach into your inner flame and cup a fragment of it in your hand. Carefully join your inner flame with the candle flame. (Once you get used to seeing your inner flame, then you can light the outer candle with the outer flame and inner flame at the same time).

As you look at the candle flame with your inner vision, the flame grows bigger until it is big enough for you to step into. Step into the flame and let the flames lick around you. They do not burn you; they cleanse and refresh you as you bathe in the sacred element. You stay in the flame for a moment, enjoying its power and bathing in the flame of life. When you are ready, step forward through the flame and you will find yourself within the void. This is a place out of time, a place with no movement, no sound, no time. As you drift in this place you allow your daily life to fall away until it is the eternal you that drifts in this special place. You feel the potential of all things in this quiet space and you feel the stillness within yourself.

You form an intent in your mind to venture into the inner world of the land. With that intent, you step forward out of the void and find yourself on ground, with a slight wind in your face. You find yourself on the edge of tall forest where the trees seem to stretch up to the clouds. The forest is silent except for the sound of running water and as you look around, you find a small stream that weaves its way through the forest. You follow the water as it weaves in and out of the ancient trees, and you feel as if you are being watched as you walk. The deeper you get into the forest, the more your body reacts to the surroundings. You recognize certain scents and long buried memories flit in and out of your mind, but they do not stay with you long enough for you to fully grasp what it is you are remembering. The more you walk, the deeper your memory of this place becomes, and the more of your everyday life falls away.

Eventually the stream tumbles into a clearing and you step into the light after the darkness of the forest. Before you is an image of intense beauty. An ancient gnarled and twisted tree sits upon a small outcrop of rock and earth, which sits in a small lake of water. On the other side of the tree is a horizon with a stunning sunrise and the waters of the lake seem to cascade over the horizon and tumble down into nothing. The tree emits its own light, which shines out among the trees, and in the shadows, tiny bright beings dart and hide.

You walk to the edge of the water and put your hand in the lake. The water feels bright, full of life and power. The tree senses your presence and you can feel the tree reaching out its thoughts to you. The tree asks you to sing. You begin to sing songs that you know but as the power of the water and tree surround you, a deeper sound emerges from within you and you begin to sing the sound that is your soul. Everything around you begins to emit sound, each tree, each rock, the water, each being joins with your sound to create a wonderful harmony. Out of the forest come beings that are a part of this land, of this world, and they each have a sound too. They sing their sound and the vibrations resonate deeply with yours, and you realize that these beings are connected to you. They are ancestors of your genetic line going back millions of years but in this place there is no time: it is the eternal forest that walked across the face of the Earth.

One of the beings comes forward and touches you and allows you to touch them. You commune together, telling each other about the way you live. After the communion has ended, it is time to leave. You will be able to come back here whenever you need to, but always treat this place with respect: it is the sacred inner landscape of the planet and must be protected.

You have an urge deep within you to dive into the water, which you do. You swim towards the horizon and you find fishes swimming along side, who also communicate with you. They are the guardians of the Great Tree. You swim until you come to where the water falls into nothing and you fall with the water, through space, through time, through the void. You fall and fall, your mind peaceful as the water cascades around you. The longer you fall the more you become aware of the water all around you, traveling with you. The water seems to fall through you, joining with the water within your body, filling you with life and vitality. You lose the sense of falling, instead becoming filled with a sense of being water. Its soft silence fills you with a deep peace and floats with and all around you. Slowly you become aware of a gentle flame burning just above the water within you, and you remember your humanity. You remember the chair in which you were seated and remember the journey you have just completed. When you are ready, open your eyes.

* * *

The vision takes you into the heart of the inner landscape of our world as it is in our era, which means the last 5 million years. Obviously it would have looked very different 100 million years ago, and the inner landscape slowly shifts and changes with the Earth's surface. The inner interface of the land has many differing presentations, just like the outer landscape and the tree/lake/forest is just one of them. Working with that interface of the forest gives us a deeper connection to the trees, water and beings that are all around us. It takes us to the threshold of existence of the forest, where it flows in and out of the void and allows us to interact with the consciousness of the land at a much deeper level. Humanity historically has created animal/human images as deities in an attempt to communicate with nature. Going into the inner land itself and communing with the inner forest/water in a more natural, non verbal, non ritualized communication allows us to truly connect energetically to the land and to interact with that power at a very deep level. The inner landscape is also a natural form of egregore, an inner storage of energy for the land.

Once you are familiar with the vision, it is very rewarding to do this vision in a forest where there is water. Where I live there is old woodland with springs that emerge out of the roots of the trees, so that some trees are surrounded by water. Sitting in the silence of the woodland and doing this vision is extremely powerful and beautiful, and it has brought me much closer to the land around me. This vision connects us to the land upon which we live and helps to tune us into the Earth that we serve.

The Goddess
in the Underworld

The next vision that would make sense to follow on from the inner land is one that connects us to that part of human consciousness where the power of ancestors and deities come together. The Goddess in the cave is an ancient visionary doorway to the Underworld. A Goddess who absorbs and expresses, among other things, the female ancestral consciousness that sleeps within the land. This power is expressed in cultures around the world as a powerful and often older woman/goddess/queen who resides in an underground cave that houses a pool of water or a river. The following version is based upon the form that resides in the British Isles, but the template can be used to access the same type of consciousness in other lands and the vision, if you have true contact, will adjust and display the signature characteristics. It may take a few goes for other lands to reveal their powers, but patience works wonders. You will notice that this vision does not use the void as an access point, but goes directly into the Underworld. If you wish to follow a path of visionary magic, then eventually you will learn many ways to access the inner realms and each has its own advantages and usefulness.

The Vision of the Goddess in the Underworld

Light a candle, close your eyes and be still. With your inner vision, see a flame burning quietly within you, the flame that burns at the edge of the void. In vision, reach into your inner flame and cup a fragment of it in your hand. Carefully join your inner flame with the candle flame. As the two flames merge together, the flame grows bigger and the floor beneath the flame fades away. The flame plunges into the Underworld and you lean over to look down and watch it. As you look, you see very old and worn steep steps carved out of the side of the tunnel and you climb into the darkness, staying close to the wall as you begin to climb down. The steps pass by old roots, rocks, and sweet smelling earth as you climb deeper and deeper into the darkness. The flame has landed below and you carefully step your way down towards it.

The steps go around and around, and the light of the surface world fades into the darkness as you aim for the flame below. You come to a stop at the bottom of the tunnel and look around. The flame casts its glow that allows you to see into the darkness. To one side you see a large crack in the rock face and you squeeze yourself through into a very narrow path between. The flame follows you and together you make your way down a twisting descending path deep into the land. The flame goes ahead and after a few yards vanishes around a corner leaving you in the dark. Stretching out your arms to touch each side of the rock face, you walk carefully, feeling the floor with your feet.

The path turns a corner and a faint green light glows from a crack in front of you. Squeezing once more through a rock crack, you emerge into a cavern, the rock walls emiting a very faint green glow. To one side of the cavern is a pool of water and on the far side is an old woman sleeping in a large rock throne covered in shells. Between her and you, the floor is littered with sleeping animals, birds, bees and insects. Very quietly and carefully, you pick your way through the sleeping family to the water and wash your hands, face and mouth.

As you stand back up and turn to face the old woman you see that she has one eye open and is watching. She beckons you and holds out her hand, expecting a gift. Reach into your pocket and give her whatever appears in your hand. Once she is happy with her gift, commune with her and tell her about yourself, and the land where you live. Listen carefully to what she has to say and try to remember it. When you have both finished, thank her and then carefully pick your way back through the sleeping animals to the entrance of the tunnel. By the door is a candle flame and the old woman tells you to take it with you to light your way back. As you find the stairway, you notice for the first time that ancient carvings are etched out on the rough rock walls as you climb back to the surface. One stands out, try to remember it so that you can work with and learn about it.

As you emerge into your own world, go and sit back in your chair before the candle flame. Look at the flame and allow its stillness to wash over you. In that stillness you remember your experience, the things that were said to you and the signs, sigils or beings that you saw. Once you have recovered your memory, open your eyes and look again at the candle flame. When you are ready, blow out the flame.

* * *

The visions above are from a very specific line of magic that has been operating in the Western world for a very long time. Many of the visions from this line have been in operation for thousands of years but they are not a dogma that must be followed. They are the accumulation of many lifetimes of visionary exploration often expressed through a religious mystical line. It is important to remember that for millennia, magic was a major part of the inner mysteries of priest/ess-hoods and was tightly interwoven with the spirituality of ancient cultures. It is only since the advent of Christianity post 2nd Century AD that it became separated from spirituality and became its own path.

The reason I mention this is to ensure the understanding that ritual and vision, and the methods of operating them, are bound by the dynamics of the inner and outer worlds, not the rules and regulations of magical lines, lodges and religious paths. They are a part of our existence and as such were respected in the ancient temples for those capable of operating them. The peoples of ancient times stated that their method of ritual and vision was tied to their specific deities, not because of dogma, but because it was literally true. Their deities, rituals and magic emerged through their consciousness from the powers of the elements and land all around them. To work with a foreign method often brought magical chaos as it was designed and emerged from a very different land power. We see examples of that mismatch in today's magical practices, but I think that mismatch will slowly fade away as it catches up with our modern day mobility and melting pots.

The Egyptians give us our first record of one culture using the magic of another in the pyramid texts of the Pharaoh Unas (2450 –

2300 BCE) where proto Canaanite spells were used alongside Egyptian ones. This should not have been magical issue as the landmass from northern Syria all along the coast to Morocco shares many power similarities. But if those spells had been invoked on the British Isles at that time, it would have been a different matter entirely. It's an interesting question to see how our globalism will affect our relationships with the land and its powers, and how mobile those powers will become in light of our constant interactions with foreign lands. I know for me, certain powers from other cultures operate with me quite well on this British landmass, whereas others have failed miserably or been unstable.

2
Ritual Magic

There is one very interesting dynamic that comes into play with a lone ritual: there is no audience. Because magic demands a certain amount of imagination and creativity, it can open the door for drama queens who perceive their ritual roles as a performance and play out their little power fantasies. By doing that, the power raised by the ritual stays in the realm of psychology and doesn't move any further.

So what is happening in a ritual? Well it all depends on what you want to achieve, how you are doing it and with whom you are doing it. From an inner point of view there are a variety of kinds of ritual that all work magic in different ways and at different power levels. There are types of rituals that sustain inner patterns, rituals that create inner patterns, and rituals that tear apart certain patterns. There are rituals for the whole community, rituals for a working group and rituals done by a very small group or a sole worker. Each magical tradition has its signature ritual that is used to interface with power and work patterns, but the underlying principle is generally the same.

Group rituals

This is the most common form of ritual and usually involves a group of people and onlookers. Although it is not directly relevant to a lone practitioner, it is important to understand the dynamics of the different forms of magical ritual.

The group ritual is often a mythical re enactment that is keeping an inner path trodden and therefore open in the consciousness of the people. The large community ritual ensures an energetic link between the land/temple/deity/beings and the people. That way, the path of communication, energy and cooperation is kept open by following the ritual footsteps of those who came before us.

The main source of power in this type of ritual is in the re-enactment. By walking a path already trodden, contacts and powers woven into that original pattern are energized and interacted with. The trodden path becomes a window over the generations until it is like a program whereby you throw the switch and on it comes. From an inner point of view it is one of the weakest forms of ritual magic because although there are more people and it is a well established pattern. It is usually a dispersed form of energy work that works through the characters of the myths and is kept in a tightly humanised form. So there are stories, deities, beings and actions all represented by human players through which the power is quickly dispersed.

A more powerful form of this kind of ritual is one whereby a small group of magical mediators undertake the ritual and the community watches passively. What makes it more powerful is two things, the first being that the ritualists are not doing a drama re enactment, they are actually partaking of the original action from an inner point of view. So the action that they ritually take only happens once from an inner point of view: they are returning to the original happening. The second thing that makes this more powerful is that the community audience is drawn upon as a power source. Their passive observance allows the ritualists to draw upon the energies of all those present to create a large battery to power the ritual. This was often the case in ancient world and survived in the form of the early Catholic high mass whereby the congregation had no part in holy of holies and were merely bystanders who were there to provide energy. The mass developed over time to include the congregation more and thus dispersing the power expression that the ritual awoke.

A new form of this ritual can be established by using a mythical pattern or a newly written script and re enacting the ritual in exactly the same way each year – such consistent action builds an inner path so that power can flow through.

In more modern times, the communal ritual has also become a vessel for self-help/psychological therapy and while that is valid in itself, it is not a form of ritual magic in that it does not create an interface with an inner being or landmass and the ritualists. Instead it creates a link between the outer and inner self of the individual.

The Lone Ritual

A lone practitioner must establish, from the very beginning, a sense of focused intention and stillness so that the method of ritual is established from the very beginning with a sense of integrity with no showmanship. Although such an undertaking is very difficult for someone working on their own trying to learn, it reaps huge benefits in the future years when the practitioner has developed a strong, unique and focused skill of ritual pattern making.

The first thing that is important in a ritual is to know the physical directions in the space and to be clear about where you are working in and why. The reason for this is that each direction has a certain quality of power that flows through it and that will affect your work. The definitions of directional powers vary according to which tradition or magical method is being used, but in the northern hemisphere it is generally expressed as - air/utterance/sword/religions of the book in the East, fire/wand/creativity/ solar religions in the South, water/ emotions/cups or vessels and religions of the waters or Moon in the

West, and earth/land/death and religions of the Underworld in the North.

Of course there are variants upon these themes such as the magic of Egypt placed death in the West, the desert where the Sun sets. Some magical systems place the sword in the south, probably in reference to the aggressive nature of most solar religions and deities. I suppose that the sword would be at home in either east or south as in the east it brings through the power of justice and focus, and in the south the powers of battle and war. On top of such variants is the fact that the powers in the directions can be very fluid at times, and have elements of each of the four powers within themselves. It can get very confusing so I feel the best approach is to work with one pattern until you are completely at home and once that foundation is laid down, you can begin to experiment and explore. A very important point to remember is that the powers that flow through the directions are not a consequence to your attributions, but are expressions of the land upon which you live. If you persist in trying to impose a pattern of power upon a direction that does not mediate that power in a balanced way then you will have disharmony that will ultimately sabotage your work.

For example, in one place where I worked magically for a while, there were springs to my west, but the power that flowed out of those springs was not healing or emotive power, but were powers of female warriors. No matter what work I was doing, if I worked in the west, a very powerful female warrior presence made herself known in no uncertain terms. So that was the power I worked with in the west. You have to be flexible and able to adjust your work to enable natural patterns of power to flow. That ability does not come easily, but will emerge in your consciousness once you have established patterns and are able to feel powers flowing back and forth. If you are working with the wrong power in the wrong direction, you will be made aware of that fact.

Altars

Altars are for working on, they are not a New Age store display, and so it is best not to fill them with tons of magical crap. It is vogue these days to use an altar as an expression of your self and your beliefs, so they are filled will statues, trinkets, crystals and all sorts of products. Altars are thresholds for power and communication, if you fill them with tat, the streams of contacts and powers will be confusing, fragmented or may even block the work. Again it is all about the glamour. If you want to do a magical display, fine, do it on your dresser, but leave your altar as a clear working space with only the essential items upon it.

Those essential items would be: the element which you use as a focus and doorway i.e. a candle flame, or a bowl of water, or a rock, whatever magical implement you are using i.e. sword/wand etc, and any object that is directly relevant to what you are currently doing i.e. paper inscribed with sigils, ancestral bone etc. If you wish to work only in relation to a particular deity then an image or statue of that deity will be on there too. One word of advice, if the altar has a deity upon it, then it is the domain only of that deity and nothing else. Any work that is not directly related to that deity can be blocked by the narrow field of contact it can invoke. This is where the separation of devotion and pure magic comes in. One suggestion that has worked well for me is if you are working with a particular deity, have an altar just for them and then have a magical working altar that is separate.

If you can keep the same table/surface for an altar then that will help to build up the patterns and focus the power. However if you cannot, then an altar cloth that is used only for magical work can suffice. There are also methods for working magic using floor patterns and no altar, which again is about the establishment of patterns in a space. It can be a bit difficult though if you need to use implements. Once the techniques for opening, closing, mediating and raising power are well established, and the magician has good focus, then an inner flexibility emerges whereby you can work anywhere, anytime, and eventually without any implements or tools. But first the rules need to be learned so that they can be thrown away.

Implements

The traditional way to acquire one's magical implements is a way that very rarely occurs these days in the rush to consume and have everything you want when you want it. It would often take many years to acquire the implements, and they would come one at a time when the path of power that the implement mediates crosses yours. Sometimes the implements would come into a magician's life before they had decided to study magic and it would stay with them, quietly ticking away in the background until they finally realized what it was.

The sword would be given/come to a person after they had learned the lesson of justice, and had acted with honour in the best way that they could in a dangerous situation. Once the person had done all that they could for themselves, the sword would arrive as back up, protection and as a teacher. The wand arrives always in unusual circumstances and heralds the path of learning about fire/solar magic. The cup is given to the magician as a token of love and not necessarily erotic -it can be any form of love. It can also appear as a cauldron of regeneration, appearing when the magician is in a place of needing regeneration after battle or is about to undertake service to heal others. The shield, which can also be a rock, bone, or sigil, teaches protection, the land and your place upon the land, and again turns up when you have exhausted your ability to defend yourself in an honorable way. From this you can see why such a method was not fashionable and was cast aside.

Methods changed with a need to acquire the implements as part of the rigid structures of magical grades that became very fashionable through the influence of Freemasonry. Texts were written with formalised ways of making and finding your magical implements so that the magician, not magic, had control over the pace of their magical development. In today's world there are many variants upon the theme with courses, books and workshops that show you how to make/find and consecrate your implements, down to the all out commercial 'get it all here' occult shops.

To find a sense of balance with magical implements, I feel a good way forward in today's world is to give fate a chance to put these implements in your path, but also to be pro active. Flow with the momentum of magic rather than against it by slowly building up your four implements over time starting with one and working around the directions/elements with the one implement working in each direction and the centre. So a budding magician would first perhaps find a sword and begin to work with it until they have got a very good understanding as to how it works. Not only does that stop the gluttony of wanting it all at once, it allows a person to work in depth with one line of power so that they have an excellent grounding before they move on to the next implement.

Don't feel that you have to work to a rigid rule of developing your implements in step with the rule book of which comes first and why. They work with you and draw you in when you are ready to open up to that power. In truth, you cannot force an implement to work for and with you, as the power of the implement comes partly from within. It will open within you when you are ready, not when you want it to be. This ensures that people cannot tap in the true depths of magical power that these tools hold until the practitioner is in a space where they can truly access and understand it.

My first implement arrived on my doorstep as a teenager and I had no idea what it was. It was the implement more than anything else that led me on a path of magic and it took a while before I finally realised what it was and how it worked – I can be a bit slow on the uptake sometimes. The sword turned out to be the sword of the original Golden Dawn Temple (Horus no5) from Bradford Yorkshire. Next came the cup ten years after the sword arrived and the wand appeared under very strange circumstances twenty two years after the sword first made its appearance. My shield only turned up a year ago, some thirty years after the sword.

What I did discover over the years is that the actual implement itself is not as important, as the power within that implement. That power, once it has appeared properly in your life can be transferred out of one physical implement into another. So you may have more than one sword over your lifetime, but the power that resides in those various swords is one and the same. The transfer is a technique to protect the power should something happen to the implement itself. Another quirk is that the implements change as you do and as your knowledge and understanding of implements deepens, so the instruments and tools of your craft change and transform. So for example when your work with say a wand gets to a deeper level, often it will break and another one, that has a deeper and more profound expression of power will cross your path. Sometimes the transfer of power is automatic, and sometimes initiated by the practitioner.

Working with the implements

Different traditions have variants upon the theme of magical implements, of how they work and what you do with them. It is pointless for me to go into any depth on the different traditional methods as I do not have working experience of every tradition out there, and I do not write about things in theory, only in practice. It is also important to note that just because you have the implement, does not mean that you will learn its secrets straight away. In truth, learning the true power and purpose of a tool can take many years and may evade understanding throughout a lifetime. But the best way to move forward is to begin working in a disciplined way with the tool and the more experience you gain, the more flexible you become in your working methods. It is at that point that the tool can truly begin to commune with you and teach its power. But it is vitally important to establish a pattern of work with boundaries first, so that you can learn within a contained field. Those that try to dive in to it all straight away either fail to penetrate the power, or if they are naturally very talented, will learn a great deal but in a very harsh way that could permanently damage them.

Magical implements are used in roughly two forms, ceremonial and magical. The ceremonial use of implements in magical ritual is where the sword, cup, wand and shield are used in a representative way. So the sword etc takes up a ritual function that represents an action or power connected to the powers/deities that the ritual centers around. This is true for 50% of magical ritual paths, and also includes various forms of witchcraft, religions etc.

The magical use of an implement is where it i.e. sword etc is 'awakened' by a consecration that merges it with the original magical 'sword'. The consecrated implements do not represent anything; they are working members of the team and contribute power, knowledge and contact to the ritual. The following descriptions of the implements list not the representational aspects of magical implements, which can be found anywhere in books, but the magical consecrated details that are found in the wide spectrum of the Western Mysteries.

The Sword

The power of the sword is something that has a deep resonance with the lands of the United Kingdom, along with the stone and cup or Grail. Legends of magical or sacred swords reach far back into Irish, and British history. One of the re occurring themes is the fact that the sword is not to be wielded in battle, but held in justice or sovereignty. In magical terms, the sword is present in the ritual as a fellow worker and a focus of power, or as a guardian, or used to confer sovereignty, power or consecration. It is not wielded in the sense of a weapon but used for consecration. There are also times where the sword has been consecrated and enlivened to become a window for a particular being. In such a case, just the unsheathed presence of the sword is enough to affect a power flow and influence a ritual. When a magical sword has become a consecrated window, it is very important not to wield that sword as a tool: it is not a tool but a being, usually very powerful and able to create disaster if misused.

The Wand

The wand is usually a branch of a tree, and holds the power of that tree for the use in magical ritual. It can also be one of the tools of kingship, with its connection to the Royal Oak of Britain. The consecrated wand, from a sacred tree is like the sword, a being in its own right and is most often used as a focus tool. The intent of the magician in the ritual is focused to a fine point, which is then galvinised into action in some cases by the directional use of the wand.

The Cup

Using the cup in ritual when it has been consecrated affects the fluid that is placed within. It is used for blood, wine, water, and as a consecrated vessel, brings about transformation to the fluids within the cup. Traditionally in magic, the cup is associated with womanhood, the womb and love. In actual magical practice I have not found this to be the case. What I have found, working with a variety of consecrated vessels is that the cup is connected to powers that regenerate warriors, like the cauldron of regeneration. I live in an area of many cold springs and I have found that the power of these springs is more akin to the powers of Valkyries than it is to love and motherhood. So where the sword and wand can work as actual beings, I have not personally found that with the cup, however used properly, it is a very powerful tool of transformation.

The Shield

Just as it sounds, the shield is there to protect, hide and deflect. A consecrated shield will protect you from things that you cannot cope with, but it will not blindly do this in the way an unconsecrated shield would. That is good. Too much protection is a dangerous thing in magical work and an intelligent shield can add to the power of a ritual without putting you in long-term danger from over confidence. Five years ago I would have maintained that magical shields are not beings but tools. I changed that stance after a shield came to me that is very much a sacred being, fierce, powerful and its own boss. In ritual it is there as a worker, doing its job without interference from me or anyone else. It blocks certain streams of damaging power and acts as a power storage unit, holding power until it is needed.

As always with such powerful things as consecrated objects, you can only learn so much from another person or book; you will truly learn the qualities, consciousness and powers of implements by long-term use and observation. I used to be very sure of myself and make pronouncements about certain tools and powers, but over the years practical long term experience has shown me that our understanding of magic in all aspects is extremely limited and we will never be able to properly quantify, control or pronounce certainties about it. So anything that is read in this or any other book is a fraction of the truth of magical power and should be used as a guide until one gets to the stage where you have learned the rules, the powers and are beginning to walk your own path.

The Basic Attunement of Ritual Tools

A basic attunement of ritual tools is a simple contacted tying in of the ritual tool to the inner powers that work through ritual implements. It is the run of the mill magical sword, cup, wand and shield set up and the attunement methods tie in the magical power needed for the implements to work properly. It is not a consecration of magical implements, but it is a step in that direction. In the early days of magical training, it is much better to work with attuned magical tools first so that you can gain a good understanding of how and why they work, before you progress to working with consecrated tools. The various methods of consecration of magical tools are discussed in the book *Magical Knowledge III – The Contacts of the Adept*.

The first thing to note is that when you get an implement ready to attune, you cannot pre judge what direction it is going to work. To try, even at an advanced level of work, to impose a pattern or action on a magical implement is sheer folly. It is important to understand right from the beginning that although there are particular attributes in Western magic given to specific directions, in truth all the directions and their powers are fluid and the inner contacts connected to the implement will more or less choose which direction you will work in. Sometimes the implement will be worked within a traditional direction, but sometimes an instrument will gravitate towards a direction it would not normally be connected with.

The following method can be used for any of the four implements tools and will connect it to an inner contact, which will mediate power from the inner direction to the implement. Whichever directional power you work with, that is what will flavor the magical tool's power. To gain the basic skills needed to undertake such a working, if you are not used to ritual while also using vision, it would be a good idea to practice some of the basic exercises that are listed later in this chapter. They will give you a deeper understanding of how vision and ritual come together in the simplest terms, and will give you a chance to develop the necessary focus needed to attune objects.

Basic Consecration Method

First cover the ritual object in dry salt and leave overnight. In the morning, recite the exorcism and blessing of substance over the tool (see Appendix 2).

Have four altars set up and a fifth altar or freestanding candle in the centre of the room. Each altar should have a candle upon it and nothing else. Starting in the east, go to the altar and stand quietly before the candle. Feel yourself stilling and connecting to a silent flame burning at the edge of the void. When you are ready, using your inner vision, reach inside of yourself to your own deep inner flame, and cup a fragment of the flame upon your hand. Use this inner flame to light the inner candle and once the inner candle is lit, then light the outer candle.

Stand before the flame and close your eyes. Using your imagination, see beyond the flame and see a gateway on the otherside of the altar. Using your inner voice, ask for an inner contact to come to the threshold of the east to assist with work, and see the gates slowly swing open. You will see a priest or priestess slowly walking towards you and they stop at the threshold of the gates, which is also the threshold of the altar. Thank them for being here, and then walk to the south. Repeat the action in the south, the west and the north until all four directions are lit and there is an inner contact in each direction waiting to work with you.

Light the central candle, which is the flame at the centre of all being, and then pick up the ritual tool you want to consecrate. Instead of going to the traditional directions for that tool (i.e. west for cup etc), starting in the east, go to the altar and place the tool on the altar and then place your hands upon the tool. See how the tool feels. Pick up the tool and hold it over the flame to the inner contact priest or priestess who is waiting for you and ask them if this tool is the tool for that direction, are they willing to work with it? They will say either yes or no. You may not get a definitive answer straight away, in which case you move onto the next direction. If all four directions are undefined in their answer, then you go around again. Another method of choosing the directions is to simply walk up to each direction holding the tool. You will either be attracted or repelled in the various directions. Either way one direction will really stand out for that tool.

When you have chosen the right direction, take it to the altar and hold it over the flame. The priest/ess will place a hand over the object or they will take it from you and do something to it. If they place a hand upon it, place your hand over their hand and feel a power passing from them, through you and into the object. This process will take a long or a short time, there is no way to tell beforehand. Once they have finished, place the object on the altar and go out of the room: the inner contacts need clarity to complete the power transfer and it is easier and better if there are no humans in the room. The power is all passed by touch and resonance.

You will get a very clear indication of when the object has been completed, and at that point go back into the room, and starting in the east, say thank you to the inner contact for their work. Let them withdraw, close the gates in your mind, and blow the candle out. Repeat this in the other directions and lastly in the centre.

* * *

Now you must learn to work with the implement. It will be a combination of its traditional use plus the quality of the direction that it was worked in. It is also possible that a being was placed in the object by the priesthood, but if so it will be very obvious right from the start. A good way of learning about the tool is to open the direction it has been tuned to, and go through the gates in vision with the object in your hand with the intention to commune with the priesthood of that direction: they will teach you all that is possible for you to learn about working with your tool.

The difference between learning and working

This is one of the biggest steps in understanding that seems to evade many schools of magic these days, learning and doing. Many lodges have descended into training schools whereby only a small amount of adepts within the lodge actually do continuous work. The practice methods become the 'be all and end all' of practical magical technique, for example the practice of summoning a being. A being is summoned, under terrible strain of work only to be instantly dispatched. Why I ask? So they can learn to banish it.

Such methods belong in a different era, in the days when the extremes of good and evil dominated the human consciousness. It stinks of fear, rudeness and ignorance by today's standards. Magic is a part of us, therefore our understanding of magic changes with the maturation of the culture and the individual. Such a method shows fear and a need to dominate a being, with no learning of anything about the being, rather the magician refers back to books written many years ago. And don't forget, just because it's published doesn't mean it's true.

In today's so called enlightened era, magicians should be more prepared to venture into the domain of other beings with respect and caution, to find a deeper understanding of what those beings are, how they operate and their boundaries. Such an approach gives one a great deal more information regarding the banishment or removal of such beings should that become necessary.

The line between learning and working has become entwined and it is healthier for all concerned if the clear distinctions are followed. The main reason is that certain methods are specifically put together to teach the magician a great deal without killing them and to instill a healthy working practice. Work however, although often packed with learning experiences (you never ever stop learning), is often dangerous, exhausting and pushes the magician to the mental, emotional and physical limits of his/her ability.

Basic ritual patterns and exercises

The following is a series of exercises, starting with the simplest, that will train a person in the basics of pattern making, and prepare them for deeper ritual skills. The following methods are the ones that I often used to train beginning magicians, and although there are many different ritual paths with their own methods, these are the ones I know best. As I have said before, I never put anything in a book that I have not done so that what I pass on is all tried and tested for a long time. There are too many instances these days where people work from texts that were copied from other texts that were copied from another book somewhere. That is not a healthy way to learn magic!

Instead of laying out actual rituals for people to try, I have pulled together a series of exercises that train the magician in the inner power dynamics of how energy moves around, how contacts actually work and what is happening from an inner point of view when the magician recites during ritual. If the outer ritual has no inner power base, then it is just a drama display with wishful thinking. However, if the inner energy and contact dynamics are learned first, then when the magician actually comes to performing a ritual, and uses the inner techniques that are learned in these exercises, then the ritual becomes a major power action.

The following working methods and suggestions are not a hard fast rule but they are from a system that works well. Once you have understood what is actually happening in these exercises and tasks, then the underlying principle can be grafted onto any other system which you feel draws you the most. The reason for this is that the methods are magical techniques, not magical dogmas from a particular path.

Opening and closing directions and working spaces

This is the first skill that is needed to develop magical sensitivity of the veils between the worlds, and to be able to wake up and put to sleep the magical space. In a deeper truth, a space cannot really be closed down from the inner worlds, it doesn't really work that way, but barriers can be put up and lines drawn. On a surface level these act as closings and openings. But if a powerful being, humans included, wanted to get into the inner space of a magical temple, if they were skilled enough it would be almost impossible to keep them out by using a closing of a space. More powerful and ingenious methods would be needed. I tell you this only to ensure that a) you get a reality check about magical abilities versus powerful beings, and b) that you also get a deeper understanding about how space actually works.

The opening and closing of a magical space creates a 'tuning' frequency so that the room, the land and any attendant beings prepares for what is about to happen. It is like focusing a lens. By changing the frequency of a space any inner 'static' from the building or passers by, human and otherwise, gets tuned out. The room and the person working in the room moves from an everyday to a different 'working' frequency. The outer effect is that the space becomes quiet and the people working become 'invisible' to casual passers by. The more this is built upon, by regularly opening and closing in a specific space, the more the room becomes tuned. I stopped closing my dedicated working spaces many years ago, for a variety of reasons, which allowed a certain tuning to develop within that space that became deep and profound. Such depth provides its own deep protection and makes the work invisible to all but those on the same frequency. Other people who work in the same tradition, or who are naturally psychic will pick up on the space as they walk past: they will 'feel' the silence.

The opening of the space method is simple and yet becomes very profound the deeper the magician goes into the inner realms. Remember this profundity when you execute this method: have respect for its simplicity, which will allow it to open out the true depths of power hidden in this simple action.

The action needs a candle and a box of matches. Preferably you can work with an altar, but it is not needful.

Before you light the candle, stand in total silence and stillness. Close your eyes and see with your inner vision. From that stillness pass into the void and deepen that stillness within yourself. Feel yourself losing the boundary of your body and have a sense of your spirit spreading out through space. Once you are deep within the void, see a flame in the distance come slowly from the depths of the void towards you. When closer, see your own inner flame resonate within you. Reach within yourself for a fragment of the flame and cup it in your hands. Light the inner candle flame and then open your eyes, staying in the void, and light the outer flame. Stand before the flame for a moment with eyes open but still in the void. See the power of the void spill out of the flame into the room until you and the room are in the void.

* * *

That action, when built up over time, can become extremely powerful and useful in many ways. It should be obvious why the use of visionary training is very important right from the very beginning. The two, vision and ritual, are inextricably linked in higher magic and they balance out power to make it more manageable.

The next step is to tune the directions. Magical work can be done through an almost limitless list of directional patterns. Most traditions have their own direction pattern of one sort or another. Some are more obvious that others. For example the use of the pentacle shape would be a five directional pattern, and many witchcraft groups use a fourfold directional pattern to denote the elements and seasons. I use either one, two, four or five depending on what I am doing. Some people work with a seven directional pattern – the four directions, the centre, above and below. I'm not too sure about the validity of such a patterning, which I have used myself, as a definite ritual. The directions of above and below cannot be worked with physically (you cannot put candle, altar etc there) so it is down to vocal recognition of the direction (which is not the same as ritual patterning) and the use of inner vision without physical ritual interaction or implements, which immediately bring about an imbalance of the flow of power between inner and outer expressions. That does not mean that above and below are not worked with; rather it means that those two directions are approached as realms, which they are

(Underworld and Overworld) as opposed to part of a physical ritual pattern direction. It is very important to ensure that you are always very clear about what it is you are doing, who is where and what is happening.

Creating a directional space

Just for the sake of training I will do this exercise in a five directional pattern. This pattern acknowledges the inner powers of the land around us. Once this is learned and worked with ease, then directional patterns that do specific jobs can be attempted. By using a foundation like this, good skills are learned from the very beginning that will help the magician learn how to move power around from A to B, and how to open doors deep into the inner worlds while retaining a conscious presence in our own realm.

Set up the space with a candle in each of the four directions and one in the centre. They can be on altars, boxes or on the floor. Make sure the path to each candle is clear and that you have a long taper. Ensure the phone is turned off the door locked, pets out etc.

Light the candle in the centre of the room, using the method that takes you into the void. Once the flame is established, take a flame of the taper from the centre flame, go to the east and stand before the candle. Again be aware of the void and be still. When you are still, light the candle with the taper, and 'see' with your inner vision, the inner flame settling on the candle. Do the same in the south, west and north, ensuring each time that you take the flame from the centre. The world flows in and out of the void and the directional patterning reflects that through the centre candle.

Once all candles are lit, sit in the east facing the east candle. Be still and allow the power of that direction to flow to you. It will be very faint at first and it usually takes a great deal of practice for it to become discernable. Repeat the same exercise in each of the four directions and then the centre. The more you do this, the more you will become aware of how different the powers are in each direction. When you are ready to close it down, start again in the east, be still, using inner vision, see yourself take the inner flame back into yourself and then blow the candle out. Repeat the action in the south, west, and north. Finally stand before the central flame, take the inner flame back into yourself. Be aware of the void within you and of the flame burning within the void. The two flames become one. Then gently blow out the central flame. If possible this exercise should be done daily or at least a couple of times a week so that you can really build up the inner connection with the directions and their powers.

Bringing in inner contacts to the directions

Once you have established the directions, the next phase of development both of the room and your training is to learn how to open the thresholds for an inner contact. This will not work straight away unless you are a natural medium; it is something that has to be built up in the room and within yourself. If you are working with someone who has worked with contacts for a long time, the resonance of working with a contacted magician opens out the connection within you. This is one of the sad facts for lone magicians: most skills in magic are passed on through resonance. But you can develop the skill within yourself with hard work. That work includes practicing opening the thresholds and reaching over for a contact.

If you work regularly with the lighting of the flame and opening the directions, and then reaching for the contacts using inner vision will build up a pattern within the space that will slowly attract them.

The contacts reached for in this exercise are safe and educational. Do not be tempted to reach for your own idea of a contact, or a being that you have read about: to do such work requires a great deal of inner skill that only comes after years of work. Yes you may be able to reach those contacts, but you will not be able to control how they operate in your space or easily get rid of them. You also leave yourself open to parasitical beings that will immediately latch on and will be hard to get rid of. Learn with patience, which will give you a strong and clean foundation. This method uses visionary techniques to establish contact, then worked with ritually.

Light the candle flame in the centre of the room and tune it to the void and your flame within. Using inner vision while walking around, take the inner flame from the centre and light the inner candle on the altar of the east while physically lighting the outer candle using a taper lit from the flame in the centre of the room. Do the same in the other directions working clockwise e/s/w/n. Once all the directions are lit, go back to the east. Stand with both hands upon the altar, or out if there is no altar. The candle is the threshold between the worlds: with eyes closed, using your inner vision, look through the candle flame and see beyond it the faint details of the inside of an ancient building with columns. Most of the room is obscured by mist. Call with both your inner and outer voice for a teacher or contact of the sacred utterance. Focus your vision on the mist and slowly a person will emerge on their side of the candle looking at you. Tell them in your mind who you are and that you want to learn the skills of the mysteries. Then physically put your hand beyond the flame and into their realm. They may touch your hand or make some sort of physical contact. Once you have made contact and told them why you are there, ask them if they will be willing to work with you over a period of time. If they agree, fix their image in your mind: their visual description will be what enables you to re-establish contact in the future. The contact may ask you to cross the threshold and if they do, you will step over into what looks like the courtyard of a great temple with large doors, beyond which is the great library. Do not go any further for now, but concentrate upon building up the visuals of the contact. Once this is steady, you can pass through the great doors and encounter the learning and the contacts who reside in that great temple.

When you are ready, thank the contact for being there and step back from the candle. Circle the room clockwise so that you walk and acknowledge the south, west and north flames. When you come back to east, bow to the threshold, close your eyes and take the flame back into yourself, and blow it out. Repeat the same in the south, west and north. Finally stand before the centre, take the flame into yourself and blow it out. The flames all merge with your inner flame, which in turn merges with the void.

* * *

It may take a few goes until you 'see' a contact with your inner vision, as it is a difficult thing to do. Some people never see but sense and 'feel' a contact. That is fine; just remember the 'feeling' of that particular contact and use it as a way back to them when you next work in the direction. It is something that needs to be built up and the more you work with it, the stronger the contact will become. You are using your imagination to build a window that a contact can step through. The basic image is taken from your imagination but it is not random. It is a quite complex inner procedure that in itself is quite fascinating. The inner and outer lighting of the flame with intent is the first step. That lights up the flame in the inner worlds. The intent behind the lighting creates a particular frequency that begins to narrow the field of contact. The use of a specific image, for example the ancient building with columns, tells the inner worlds that you are looking for a contact of the ancient temple mysteries, that way any inner being picking up on your flame knows your intentions. Using your imagination to form a human figure out of the ancient buildings narrows the field of contact even more to a human of the mysteries operating within an ancient building (temple).

That focusing of the lens through thought and intent creates a tunnel for a contact of the mysteries that is willing to work with humans. The contact will use your inner image to dress itself, so that you can interact. Once you have a solid working connection with the power in the east, it will be time to approach a contact in the south.

Contacts in the South

The visionary steps used in each directional working begin in the same way, and overall are very similar; the aim is to develop a specific working method that builds over time.

Light the candle flame in the centre of the room and tune it to the void and your flame within. Using inner vision while walking around, take the inner flame from the centre and light the inner candle on the altar of the east while physically lighting the outer candle using a taper lit from the flame in the centre of the room. Do the same in the other directions working clockwise e/s/w/n. Once all the directions are lit, go back to the south. Stand with both hands upon the altar, or out if there is no altar. The candle is the threshold between the worlds. With eyes closed, using your inner vision, look through the candle flame and see beyond it the faint details of the inside of a circular space with a fire in the centre. Most of the area around the fire is obscured by mist. Call with both your inner and outer voice for a teacher or contact of the sacred flames.

Focus your vision on the mist and slowly a person emerges and stands on their side of the candle looking at you. Tell them in your mind who you are and that you want to learn the skills of the mysteries. Then physically put your hand beyond the flame and into their realm. They may touch your hand or make some sort of physical contact. Once that contact is made, step over the threshold and you will find yourself walking to a circular space within a clearing or a building where there is a fire or flame in the center, and priests/esses around the flame. Go to the central flame and reach within yourself. Cup a fragment of your inner flame and add it to the central flame. Once you have done this, step back and the contact that you made will reach into the fire and give you a fragment The exchange of fire connects you deeply to the fire at the centre of all flames in the south and will give you a connection with the priesthood in this direction.

The priest will lead you back to the threshold of your altar and the contact will work with you both at the threshold and in the direction.

When you are ready, thank the contact for being there and step back from the candle. Circle the room clockwise so that you walk and acknowledge the west, north and east flames. When you come back to south, bow to the threshold, close your eyes and take the flame back into yourself, and blow it out. Repeat the same in the west, north and east. Finally stand before the centre, take the flame into yourself and blow it out. The flames all merge with your inner flame, which in turn merges with the void within.

* * *

The contacts in the circular space are a template of inner contact for the many different priesthoods who are connected with fire power and working with them in a non cultural or heavily formed way will allow you to learn basic skills without agendas.

Contacts in the West

Light the candle flame in the centre of the room and tune it to the void and your flame within. Using inner vision while walking around, take the inner flame from the centre and light the inner candle on the altar of the east while physically lighting the outer candle using a taper lit from the flame in the centre of the room. Do the same in the other directions working clockwise e/s/w/n. Once all the directions are lit, go back to the west. Stand with both hands upon the altar, or out if there is no altar. The candle is the threshold between the worlds.

With eyes closed, using your inner vision, look through the candle flame and see beyond it the faint details of a lake with a small island in the centre. Most of the lake and surrounding forest is obscured by mist. Call with both your inner and outer voice for a teacher or contact of the sacred waters. Focus your vision on the mist and slowly a person emerges and stands on their side of the candle looking at you. Tell them in your mind who you are and that you want to learn the skills of the mysteries. Then physically put your hand beyond the flame and into their realm. They may touch your hand or make some sort of physical contact. Once you have made contact and established why you are there, ask them if they will be willing to work with you over a period of time. If they agree, fix their image in your mind: their visual description will be what enables you to re-establish contact in the future. You may cross the threshold and stand upon the edge of the waters briefly to gain a feeling of the power that resides there.

When you are ready, thank the contact for being there and step back from the candle. Circle the room clockwise so that you walk and acknowledge the north, east and south flame. When you come back to west, bow to the threshold, close your eyes and take the flame back into yourself, and blow it out. Repeat the same in the north, east and south. Finally stand before the centre, take the flame into yourself and then blow it out. The flames all merge with your inner flame, which in turn merges with the void within.

* * *

Contacts in the North

Light the candle flame in the centre of the room and tune it to the void and your flame within. Using inner vision while walking around, take the inner flame from the centre and light the inner candle on the altar of the east while physically lighting the outer candle using a taper lit from the flame in the centre of the room. Do the same in the other directions working clockwise e/s/w/n. Once all the directions are lit, go back to the north. Stand with both hands upon the altar, or out if there is no altar. The candle is the threshold between the worlds.

With eyes closed, using your inner vision, look through the candle flame and see beyond it standing stones surrounded by mist. Call with both your inner and outer voice for a teacher or contact of the sacred standing stones. Focus your vision on the mist and slowly a person emerges and stands on their side of the candle looking at you. Tell them in your mind who you are and that you want to learn the skills of the mysteries. Then physically put your hand beyond the flame and into their realm. They will maybe touch your hand or make some sort of physical contact. Once you have made contact and established why you are there, ask them if they will be willing to work with you over a period of time. If they agree, fix their image in your mind: their visual description will be what enables you to re-establish contact in the future. Once the contact has been made, step over the threshold to find yourself in a dark cave with a priestess in the half shadows. Tell the priestess that you are there to learn about the powers of the north and commune with her.

When you are ready, thank the contact for being there and step back from the candle. Circle the room clockwise so that you walk and acknowledge the east, south and west flames. When you come back to north, bow to the threshold, close your eyes and take the flame back into yourself, and blow it out. Repeat the same in the other directions working clockwise. Finally stand before the centre, take the flame into yourself and blow it out. The flames all merge with your inner flame, which in turn merges with the void within.

* * *

Establishing the contacts and the pattern of ritual behavior in the room builds the ability to work in a contacted as opposed to a non-contacted ritual. The difference is that in a non-contacted ritual, you work ritual patterns, read invocations and enact ritual movement in order to achieve a specific aim. Sometimes the ritual intent is to bring a being or deity into the space for communication.

In a contacted ritual the practitioner opens the ritual and invites the contacts from one or all of the directions to assist at the threshold between the worlds. It commences as normal while communicating with the contacts as if they were officers in the ritual. A third form of ritual in this particular stream of work is the combination of the inner and outer: this is where a contacted ritual is conducted both in the outer and inner world simultaneously. I will talk about that later. Before I go any further with the ritual techniques, I want to cover certain issues regarding contacts.

Inner contacts and their issues

When you work with the above pattern of contact , you will be tapped into a series of lines that are very much about learning and guidance. The contacts from these directional patterns tend to be fairly straight forward in their dealings with our world. However if you do branch off in search of other contacts, ensure that what you are reaching for is a known quantity i.e. if you are interested in Setian priests, then reach for that contact (south or east probably) through the directional work. But don't just call for anyone… use you're common sense and do not invite a passer by into your work.

If a contact becomes demanding, wants blood, worship, your energy etc, then back off; you have probably picked up on a very intelligent cross dressing parasite that wants dinner. They are very clever and will show and tell you what you want to know in return for a dinner, but like all unhealthy beings, they tend to be greedy and once you give willingly, they will take more than you can afford to give. If the contact presents as very grand, showy and all powerful deity/ teacher/wise being, then chances are it is also dressing up. Inner contacts tend to be down to earth, have a strange sense of humor, do not dress up in grandeur and don't demand your first born.

Deities are a different matter and you may want to think very carefully before bringing in such power in the early stages of your work. When you do begin to work with them, it is much better to work with them as working partners where they are the stronger respected one. If you get into inner contact with a deity and offer them worship, you may be in for a lot more trouble than you bargained for. They will try to take over your life, will be extremely demanding and when you wish to move on, will try to force you to stay with them.

The other thing to remember about working with inner contacts is ask questions, lots of questions and use your everyday sense to interpret the answers. Engage the same rules you use in everyday life and do not take everything at face value. A classic example of not engaging common sense was the Magical Lodge known as the SIL and one of their inner contacts called the Master of Medicine. Dion Fortune was working on various inner explorations regarding the endocrine system and the effect magic had on the body. Her Work was deep and pushed many boundaries for its time; she was never static with her contacts, but pushed constantly for more information, more learning. After she died the contact work in the lodge continued but the information that was coming through was limited in medical knowledge. The inner contact was not a doctor, but an inner adept who was able to pick out medical information from the minds of the outer SIL adepts who contacted him. The inner contact did try to convey the information they needed but because their own medical knowledge was limited, it was very difficult to go anywhere, and their minds did not have an alternative. Thus the information that contact tried to convey could not be understood and the questions asked were limited by the understanding of the knowledge of the time.

The better course of action would have been to either try and reach a medical inner contact or work with the inner contacts in the great library. So it is not just a matter of the contact, it is also how you reach for the contact and how you work with them. They are not all knowing, all wise, and you have to find a relevant contact versed in the relevant subject matter. The same applies to the inner contacts, they have to find receptive adepts or mediums that have a vocabulary or understanding capable of interpreting what they are trying to convey. For myself I have had problems on more than one occasion where a contact has tried to teach or tell me something I could not understand. I would write it (or draw it) anyhow and hope that I would one day stumble across an interpreter.

In short, when dealing with inner contacts, use your common sense and treat them the way you would an outer teacher: they are not gods, all knowing or even all good/bad; they are beings trying to convey information to an agenda which may or may not match your own.

Establishing power flows across the directions

This is the beginning of learning how to move power around, a principal skill within magic. Once you have gotten used to lighting and closing the flame in the directions, it is time to learn how to move a power from one direction to another.

This is basic magical technique that is not particularly linked to any specific tradition; it is just a method for working with power that can be adjusted to work within most ritual traditions. The basic concept of moving inner power from A to B is learned, along with how to put it into and take it out of an object. The skills can be transplanted into different magical traditions to enliven and strengthen workings. These inner skills were not written down but taught person to person, passing down the line between those who had inner ability. These days human consciousness has become far more malleable which enables a person to use exercises and patterns to build inner skills, and to train themselves.

So why would you want to move power from A to B? Ritual magic is about the changing of the inner and or outer structure/ energy or pattern of the world around us. One useful tool is the ability to move power around so that you can bring it through from the inner worlds, work with, focus and put it into something that you are doing or making. One of the other reasons for moving power around is the re balancing of a flow, or putting the energy into someone who is sick, or to raise extra power to fuel your work. The one thing to remember is that if you are handling large amounts of power, it will really hurt you physically afterwards. You will not feel it during the work, but it will hit usually the day after. Your muscles will feel as if you have worked out in the fields for 12 hours without a break, depending on how much power you were throwing around. So do bear that in mind when you decide to do such work: once you get into the stage of manipulating and working with inner power, it is hard labour.

Moving energy from one inner direction to another

This exercise is something that must be built up over a series of weeks or even months until you develop the sensitivity to what is happening. The release and movement of the energy itself is not that hard, the perception of it is. Again this is one of those things that can be triggered in someone by resonance but if you are working alone you have to build it up yourself. At the beginning of any of these exercises it is very difficult to discern what is real and what is imagined. Don't worry about that, just work at it and let the imagination create its window. You will know for certain when it has worked as your arms will hurt like hell and the day after you will be exhausted. Moving energy from one place to another is hard work. It is the same as moving boxes: the heavier the energy the harder the work, the more the muscles hurt. What is very interesting is that when you carry a heavy box, you can see how the muscles are working and why they are tired. When you move energy, although it has no physical expression that we can discern, it still seems to engage the use of the body's muscular system and thus causes exhaustion.

To begin the exercise, light the central candle using the usual method and then go around and light the four directional candles e/s/w/n. Once all four are lit, go back to the centre and be still for a moment, feeling out as to which two directions would be best to work with. Once you have decided which direction you will receive the energy from, circle the directions clockwise until you get to that direction. Be aware of the contact that you work with in that direction and using your inner vision, reach through the flame and call them in. When they appear, ask them if they would be willing to help you in this work. If they agree, put out to them and ask for the energy to be placed in your hand. Once you have it, ask the contact to which direction it should go. It might be the one you chose or a different one.

Carry the energy in your hands working clockwise around until you come to the receiving direction. Once you are there, call for the contact of that direction and when they emerge on the other side of the flame pass the energy over to them. They may give you something back to carry to another direction. When you have finished, go around the directions acknowledging the flames and contacts and one by one put the flames out starting in the east and working clockwise.

When you have mastered this technique, it is time to work without the visionary aspect. Do the working as before but do not reach for any contact in any direction, simply go to the direction, reach over the flame and verbally ask for the power of that direction to be in your hands. When you take it to the receiving direction, simply release the energy. Once the work is finished, go around the directions again and close them down one by one.

Moving energy from an inner world direction to an outer world object

This is an interesting exercise where you gather power from a direction using the above methods but instead, you release it into an outer object, which is then worked with. This exercise is training for the inner aspect of consecrating ritual objects and enlivening deity statues. Because of the impact on the human body it is important to practice; building up the power levels slowly so that the body gradually adjusts to the inflow of power. This is a really important step and must not be skipped: allowing the body to adjust to inputs of power is vitally important so that it is able to adapt. If the body is slammed by power that it has no ability to disperse, the impact on the organs can cause permanent damage.

Most times when a person begins to draw energy out of the inner realms, unless they are a natural mediator the amount of energy handled is minuscule. If you are a natural mediator, as I am, you can inadvertently pull through large amounts of energy which does wonders for the ego but causes a good deal of damage to the body, which often is permanent. I know, I was that idiot experimenting, and I sustained damage, and it was not the only time. I bumbled my way through numerous experiments in the early days, a completely unaware loose cannon, and damaged myself many times. So heed my warning and don't be the egotistical idiot I was. Youth is no excuse!

Anyhow... back to the training exercise. Go to a nearby river, field or forest and get a stone. If you live in a city, get yourself out into the country, choose a rock and bring it home. Take note of where you got it because you are going to have to take it back. When you have your stone, go to your altars and put it in the centre by the flame. Light the centre flame, light the directions and go around them tuning yourself and the altars in by visiting each , acknowledging the flames and contacts. Once each direction is tuned in and the room feels still and balanced, go back to the centre flame and pick up the stone. Hold the stone and 'feel it' with your imagination. Feel what it needs. The stone is a record holder for the land where you took it, if there is a power deficit in that area, it will reflect through the stone. Once you have established a link with the stone by sensing what it needs, go around each direction starting in the east. Pause at the altar and feel if the stone is draw to that direction. Go around each direction, you may have to go around a few times until you are sure to which it is drawn. It will be drawn to the direction that holds the power it needs.

Once you are in the direction, place the stone by the flame and reach over for the contact. Once the contact appears in your mind, tell them your intention with the stone and ask for the energy. They will hand it over the flame and you collect it in your hands. The contact withdraws and you pick up the stone and allow the energy to flow into it. Once all the power is in the stone, place it back in the centre by the central flame and leave the room with all the candles burning. This allows the inner contacts to do whatever is needed for the stone with no human interference. You will feel when it is time to go back into the room. Go around, thanking the contacts in each direction, and blowing out the candles. Leave the stone there if it will not be disturbed, and as soon as you can, take the stone back to where you found it.

Out of curiosity, go back and visit every couple of months or so and keep a record of happenings in the area. The power will unfold over a year or so. The energy, because you worked unconditionally, will do whatever is needed, good or bad. By working unconditionally, I mean not specifying anything to the contact, just whatever is needed for that area. By doing that, what was truly needed was put in the stone, be that regeneration or destruction. If you try to conditionally set the energy i.e. healing, regeneration etc, you are bypassing what the land actually needs and placing your limited human expectations upon a landscape that is beyond our comprehension.

A lot of high magic is about moving power from A to B and often not really knowing what it is doing. Past generations in magic insisted beings and powers did what they wanted, but our human understanding of how power actually works and what will happen is so limited, that it is often more productive to allow the inner contacts to do their job properly, to allow nature to do it, and to take our place in the machinery instead of being egomaniacs trying to drive something we cannot truly comprehend.

The exercise of the stone will prepare you for creating power tools, waking up sacred spaces and temples, and consecrating objects and people. The stone will require a small amount of energy and if you do it a few times with different areas, or containers of sea or river water that is returned, you will find that over time the amount of power you are given increases. This slowly builds inner muscle and enables work to develop.

The Web of Power

The inner web of power is the next phase on from moving power around and is the basis for many rituals. A well established outer ritual that follows certain patterns will automatically instigate what I call the web of power. Outer ritualists will often not be aware of it unless they are sensitive, but the practical learning of how it operates and how to consciously work with it greatly enhances the overall strength and success of ritual. It plugs the outer ritual into an inner power source to ensure all the lights go on. When conducting an outer ritual, if the ritualist is aware/consciously enacting the web of power, it will ensure that it is operating at full capacity.

A word of caution: once the skills of transfer of power have been mastered and used in ritual, you set off a large cascade of inner action/reaction, so be very careful what you use it for. If you use this method to power a ritual that attacks/destroys/heals etc purely for your own agenda, then be ready for the backwash. If you mess with higher levels of power for silly reasons (usually to fuel vendettas, revenge, to gain power/wealth/larger sex organ etc) then you will learn a hard lesson where there is no going back. It's not about punishment for doing bad, which does not happen in the inner worlds, it is about the power imbalance which will flow through and often destroy you. Because of this, most adepts do not teach these methods of working with power. I disagree... those who need this work will develop it properly, and those that get destroyed . . .well . . .it's a self-regulating mechanism: all the idiots get wiped out.

Once you have studied the structure of this inner work, then the outer ritual can be written to slip over the top of it, like clothing. Just ensure that when you do write the ritual, that it works in harmony with what the inner web of power is doing and that the sources you are calling upon in the outer ritual do actually work in harmony: you do not want to be in the middle of a ritual and have two deities break out into a marital dispute or turf war!

In this instance, we are going to work the web of power around a ritual that benefits something or someone unconditionally. It can be a stone, a bowl of water or yourself. If you use a stone or water, then the unconditional need will be for the land that you place the stone upon or pour the water on. If it is for yourself, be aware that if you get it to work, it will bring whatever is necessary for you, be that good or bad. So if you are stuck in a rut that you have not made an effort to get out of, or if you are living in a situation where you are not letting go of something, it will instigate it for you, often with very painful results. However, in the long run it will benefit you, as it is what was needed to move you along your path.

The Ritual of the Web of Power

To begin, light the flames in the centre and the four directions, and open the contacts in the four directions so that the inner contacts are present. Starting in the east, go to the direction, and ask the contact for whatever power is needed for the land or you. Hold your hand out over the flame until you feel a power begin to build in your hand. Once there, take that power, seeing it as a line of power/light/flame in your hand, and walk to the central flame, joining the line and flame using outer as well as inner hand movements. Return to the east and draw a line of power off the flame in the east and carry it with you to the south and connect it into the south flame. There should be a line of power going from east to centre and east to south.

Repeat the same action in the south, linking a line of power to the centre and also take a line of power with you to the west. Keep working until each of the four directions is connected together and to the centre. Then work in the centre. Standing before the flame with your back to the NE cross quarter, raise your arms up to the skies and call down the power of the stars above to flow down your arms and into the centre. See with your inner vision, power streaming down from above you, flowing down your arms. Place your hands over the flame in the centre and see the line of power from above connect to the central flame. Once that is connected, point your hands to the floor and call upon the power of the Underworld to flow up through you, lifting your arms up slowly and seeing lines of power drawn up from below. Once you see the lines of power in your imagination, connect them to the central flame. Place your hands on either side of the flame and see with your inner vision lines of power running from each direction, above and below, into the flame in the centre. It will look like a web of power.

See the web, and build its brightness and strength with your imagination. Once it is strong and you can feel its power (and don't rush, this stage may take time), either hold the stone into the flame (if you are working with stone) or your hands on either side of the flame, and see the stone/you connect to the centre flame. See the web of power flow and originate/finish in the stone or your own centre and stay in that vision until you strongly feel the connection.

If you are doing this work on yourself, stand for a good length of time, feeling the directions flow into you, the power reaching every part and affecting your spirit. See the central flame passing into you and joining with your inner flame until you are the centre of the web.

If you are using a stone, see the power collect within the centre of the stone and at the centre of the web. To finish with the stone, leave it in the centre by the flame, and leave all the flames burning. Go out of the room to let the stone 'cook' in the power. You will know when it is finished; and feel it all switch off. When that happens, go in, put out the directions say thank you to the contacts, collect the stone and go put it out on the land.

If you are working on yourself, sit down with your back to the central flame, touching the central altar or close to the flame if it is on the floor, close your eyes and meditate with the power all around you. Feel into the depth of the power, be still and feel it fill every corner of your body and mind. Spend as long as you like and sense when it is all finished. When you get to that point, stand and put out the lights starting in the east and finishing in the centre. See each flame seek refuge within you as the outer flame is extinguished. It would be advisable at this point to go and have a sleep so that the power can really embed itself within you without distraction.

If you are using this as an inner skeleton for a ritual, link all the flames and directions up as described, and then begin your ritual. Don't forget to close all the lines down afterwards.

Designing a ritual

Note: it is important, as a lone practitioner, to know how a group ritual is actually built and written. Once that method is understood, it is easier to convert the method for lone use, which will be discussed later.

Once you have worked with the directions and powers/contacts within them, it is time to look at the structuring of a ritual. The first thing to decide is what is the ritual for? Is it a ritual to gain something? Is it a ritual to honour or worship something? Is it a ritual to do a job? Is it a ritual to mark passage? We talked earlier about the different kinds of ritual and it is important to have a very clear idea within yourself what it is you are trying to achieve. It is also important to ensure that if you are designing a ritual that has a certain amount of key players within it, that you can actually get that amount of people to work with you. If you are a group that is established in a particular format of magic, then it is very important that the ritual is compatible with the power flow and frequency of any deities or inner contacts you work with.

The first step of putting a ritual together is not the writing of the words, but the decision regarding what directional powers you will be working with and whether you will use an altar/s. From the minute you decide the ritual pattern that will be used, the inner contacts, if you have been working with them regularly in exercise, will begin lining up. The formation of pattern and intention is the strongest trigger in ritual and everything else hangs upon those two driving forces. With the directional layout and pattern of power flow i.e. what directions are going to be used and in what order/flow, the next step is to think about what if any implements will be used and why. Ensure that everything you decide is for a magical reason, not a 'showing off'. Drama and theatre do have a place (seasonal passage for example) but for deeper more powerful rituals it becomes a major distraction and a drain on power. The choice of implements should be directly related to the job in hand and the powers that will be used.

Once all of that has been chosen, then it is time to write the ritual speeches if there is any to be used and to allocate the people to their jobs and positions. Dates can be important but I have found, purely by accident, that if you do not concentrate upon a particular date/Moon passage etc, the ritual will line itself up with all manner of star alignments. Of course if you are designing an outer ritual, say for the solstice, it must be done on the solstice. But if it is not a seasonal outer ritual, do not limit the powers of the work by trying to force timing: trying to time a ritual for a full Moon to use its power is a limited way of thinking. Set the date according to when you can get the room/people etc together; the inner contacts will do their job in nudging you to the right date.

A good example of this was a time when I was training magicians in the USA. It was time to do a consecration on a group of experienced workers and there was only one weekend in that season when we could get together. Closer to the date, the room booking fell through and we had to take another date. During that weekend, someone who was an astrologer pointed out that we were working during a massive star alignment and we all really felt its power working with us. I would never have known about it and therefore would not have lined up the ritual to use its energy. The inner flow of power ensured that we did indeed match up with the alignment so that full power was available. That has happened many many times to me over the years so I have learned not to try and control the situation too much.

If things like dates, people dropping out, room disasters happen in the run up to a major working, don't panic, there is usually a good reason for it. People will drop out or be stopped from arriving if they are not meant to be there for one reason or another . . . it's all about being flexible and going with the flow. If they are not absolutely critical for the ritual, then go on without them and improvise. Eventually you will get an inner sense about times, people etc in regards to success or otherwise in ritual situations and instinct plays a major part.

The writing of the ritual speech should be to the point without dramatic flourishes that sap energy. There can be a tendency in magical work for people to copy the over dramatic and flowery speeches of rituals from past times. There is a danger of losing concentration, and energy by feeding it into the extensive speeches and dramatic role playing that has no actual real purpose. Think very carefully about the words, tone and implications of the words. If you are talking in ritual to a being, power or deity, are you using words of worship when you are actually looking for a co-worker? If so you will confuse the situation, yourself and the being you are talking to. And that is also a very important point: when you write a ritual speech, who is it you are actually talking to and why? It's all very nice being clever with prose, using play words, clever metre etc, but that is not the point of speech in a ritual. The point of speech in ritual is to communicate directly with a power, or to state intent. If the speech does not do one of those two things, then it is a waste of time and energy. The exception to that rule is social ritual and ritual dramas.

So write your ritual speech with care and thought, use no unnecessary words or declarations and never ever say something in a contacted ritual that you do not mean or do not really intend to carry out. Contacted ritual means that there are inner powers there with you and what you say will be taken as gospel. It is not a game and if you have real contacts there, you will be held to your word to the letter.

Ensure within the writing of the ritual that there are silences so that the officers/workers can commune with the inner contacts in the directions to ensure that the ritual is fully contacted and is working at all levels. In reality, the more powerful a ritual becomes, the more silences it has until eventually, the most powerful ones are conducted in total silence. Any communion is done silently with the inner contacts and the energy is channeled through action and thought rather than word.

When you have done the ritual, it is important during the de compression time that each of the members voice their experiences and also write them down. In a contacted ritual, there is much that goes on behind the scenes and each member will often see or experience a fragment of the whole. If everyone expresses their experiences, the fragments are pulled together to show a bigger and more complete picture. It is also important to write down those experiences so that when the ritual begins to do its job, any mistakes can be gone over, any flashes of inspiration can be noted etc. It is also very common within a day or two in contacted rituals for people to forget what happened. This dynamic becomes more pronounced the more inner contacts work within the ritual. Because of this, it can become crucial that at least one person notates what happened, what people saw and felt and then later, what the results of the ritual actually were.

Designing the lone ritual

The only difference in the structure of the lone ritual is that you work with inner contacts and yourself. It is very possible to have inner contacts working in the directions for and with you, and once you have built up experience in connecting with inner contacts, it becomes a natural progression to have them working in the room with you. The major difference in rituals with inner contacts as opposed to humans is that with a human based ritual the humans interact with the inner contacts at the threshold i.e. at the candle flame that acts as a threshold signifier. In a lone ritual the inner contacts are actually brought into the room to work with you in your world.

Before I explain how that is done it is important to understand whom you are actually working with. We have looked at inner contacts earlier, but when you are building up a series of rituals for a larger purpose, the frequency of the build up can alert other types of inner contacts who will time in and work with your rituals. The more experienced you are at working, the more frequently this will happen. When the ritual is being put together and it has a major reason, as I said earlier, certain frequencies begin to flow through the inner worlds and calls for workers can go out naturally, or can be made consciously by the magician. That frequency is not only picked up by inner adepts, teachers, workers and beings, it can also be other human magicians/ adepts living in their own time and place. The result is that when the ritual commences, workers from inner worlds, outer worlds and other times come together to complete a task.

It has happened to me many times where I have been called to work and I am drawn in vision to ritual happening somewhere and I appear out of a direction to work. I have also worked many rituals within a lodge/group and had living inner contacts come who are adepts working in vision from a distance.

A digression: A good example of this is a magical consecration of adepts that was taking place in Baltimore USA. I had a sick child at home in the UK and could not fly out with my then magical partner to conduct the consecration. We usually worked as a team with me in the north and him in the south, and inner contact priests in the east and west. When the ritual commenced, I sat down in my quiet room in the UK and the adepts began the ritual. I consciously went in vision (termed astral travel to some) and took my place in the north. The 13th person seemed very bright, and to my shock immediately vanished from my vision as soon as they were consecrated. A 14th person tried to stand before me but something was wrong; they did not have the inner markings of an initiate. I challenged them and the person changed appearance and showed themselves as the land being they really were; they had tried to gate crash! A couple of hours later, my partner called to say that all had gone well, everyone had been aware of me and all 12 had been consecrated. I told him I had actually consecrated 13 people not 12. It all became very confusing. He went back to the group who were taking a lunch break and told them. One person put their hand up and related a story of a local initiate who had died during the summer, a person who was deeply magical and who would have made a great adept. Later that night, my partner called again, related the tale and asked me to describe the 13th person, which I did. The descriptions matched and I had consecrated the recently dead initiate. She will have probably gone on to become an inner worker and the consecration she received connected her into the long line of adepts that she could draw upon. It has never happened to me since but it was the most curious happening!

Constructing a lone ritual using inner contacts

The basic construction of the ritual is the same, there is very little difference until you come to the officer part. If you need input from another being, decide what direction you would need them to come from and what sort of power they wield.

So for example if the ritual is to lay the foundation or the building of a temple space, then a temple ritualist or esoteric mason would be a good inner contact to work with. When you begin writing the ritual, keep that need in mind so that you can construct an outer call into the direction (which would be east for an esoteric mason) for the inner contact to help you. The inner work that is needed to draw in such a contact is as follows: light the central candle in the working space and go into silence. Using your inner vision, walk from the central flame to the east and light the inner candle using the flame that burns within you as a fire source. Once the inner candle is lit, call through that flame into the inner direction of east for a contact to work with you in the construction of a temple. Once that is done, open your eyes and physically light the candle in the east, and outwardly utter the same request. Leave the candle for as long as you can and if it is safe to do so, keep it lit in that direction while you are designing and writing the ritual. When you do put the candle out, see the inner candle as still burning, functioning as a beacon for a worker.

When the ritual is performed, call out for that contact to come into the space and work with you. If you are successful during the ritual you will find that you know things and are prompted to say or do them, which is the inner contact nudging and guiding you. You will feel the power levels of the working space go right up as the contact adds to them. Don't forget to thank them, and offer your hand in work in return should they need it, and be aware of them as a contact when you next go to the direction they came out of. It is very difficult with inner contacts to tell if they are living somewhere in their own time or if they are true dead inner contacts. Being able to tell the difference takes a while but you will eventually be able to differentiate.

It is also possible, once you are well versed in ritual methods, to pass in vision through the directions and into someone's working space to assist them in ritual, should they request it. It is all done through visionary methods and you will get to see how the inner patterns of ritual work; it is a wonderful weaving of power with living beings as the frame, and energy as the thread.

Working with contacted Ritual

So once you have understood the mechanics behind a ritual, practiced, written and designed in exercise, what then? Well, that is the major step. So many magicians stop at the exercises and never quite make it out into the real world of magic. A contacted ritual is like a turbo boost and would be used for major jobs such as building and consecrating magical spaces/people/implements, working on large projects to do with the land, humanity, nature, social engineering etc. Dion Fortune's Battle of Britain, a magical battle to keep the esoterically driven Nazis out of the UK, was done through contacted ritual. It required immense strength both in the people conducting the ritual and also the inner contacts drawn in to protect the land. She was successful but the strain killed her. And that is a very important point: when you work with power at serious levels, your body pays a price. It is not designed to handle large amounts of inner power over a long period of time and in today's magical world, it is an issue that is still struggled with by those using such high magical methods.

The method of power distribution needs to be very carefully studied these days as we inch our way back to the levels of magical knowledge that were held thousands of years ago. Every practitioner can add to that climb back to knowledge by keeping close records of contacted work and monitoring how their body responds to large amounts of power.

Working with non contacted Ritual

In reality, once you have worked with inner contacts, there becomes no such thing as an un-contacted ritual. Once contact with the inner worlds has been made, in truth it never really ends. In the early days of working, our perceptions are not strong or tuned enough to be aware of the continuous contact but it is there, ticking away in the background. As we progress in our magical skills, so that awareness widens out and we realize that our lives are not really our own anymore and our actions are continuously guided and sometimes manipulated by inner contact of one form or another.

What actually happens is that instead of contacted versus non contacted work, what you get is intentional versus unintentional work. To explain: If you work in a ritual without calling upon, or acknowledging inner contacts/beings, and you have been working as a contacted magician, the power flows anyway and the ritual actions become empowered and contacted by the sheer focus of the magician. The difference is that you have no idea or control over who the contact is and what they are doing. They do their job and you do yours. In a contacted ritual, you call upon specific beings/contacts and ask them to partake in a particular action. So actually, the difference is intentional inclusion versus unconscious cooperation.

The deeper into magic you go and the more power you become used to handling. You will come to a point whereby the majority of magic that you use will be unconscious cooperation with beings who are all around you. You will no longer have to invoke, call upon or ask inner contacts, beings or deities to assist or guide you. Once that first layer of contact is established and worked upon, it grows until many years later you are really a form of composite being; a magician who has many eyes looking out onto the world. The beings are all around and within you, and the work you initiate becomes a joint agenda between their worlds and yours.

So how does magic leap from doing a ritual to get a girlfriend/money/curse your neighbour, to composite ritual to rebalance the flow of power through the worlds? Intention. Intention is everything and intention draws the worlds together to work with you. And that is something that many people just do not get. If you stay in the tiny world of using magic to get what you want, you will stay low powered, un-contacted and weak, the problem is you will not know that because you will not know any different. Why do you stay un-contacted and weak? Not because it is wrong, there are no morals in magic, but because it serves no one but you, therefore other beings really couldn't give a crap. (Unless they are parasites and will give you what you want so that they get to eat your energy.) The other point is that if you use magic to get what you cannot get by outer effort, then your personality gets no abrasion therefore it remains undeveloped and immature. We get our growth from adversity, so if you side step it, there is no real growth. Magic works within us by way of our imagination, our strength of personality, our inner and outer discipline and emotional stability. So you can begin to see why, if you want to be a powerful magician, the first step is to side step the silliness of trying to manipulate the world to suit yourself. End of lecture! The reason I get so verbal and repeat this so often is because I have seen so many potentially great, truly great magicians ruined by such silliness. They devolve down into trite commercial 'Merlin' types (wise Merlin, mad Merlin blah blah) and they end up bound by their own stupidity. It is a real tragedy.

3

Initiation and its issues

The question of initiation is one that always pops up when someone undertakes magical training, be it alone or with a group. To many it marks a passage, gives them status and ensures that they feel apart from normal humanity. But in reality what is an initiation? These days there are many functions attached to the title of initiate and it has as many meanings as there are magical paths. So let's go back to its original meaning, before magic was an off the shelf pre-packed role-play pastime.

Initiation in an outer sense acknowledges your commitment to the magical path. It states in an outer sense that you are a serious practitioner embarking on the long and difficult path of the mysteries. From an inner sense, the initiation marks you with the identification sigils of the magical line that you are connected to. It ensures that inner contacts, inner adepts, teachers, deities etc all know what line you belong to. The marking of initiation is often passed on to the initiate by the magus of the lodge/group, or the high priest/priestess, if it is an initiation of religion or witchcraft. It can be removed and is not a permanent marking.

But what happens if you are walking this path alone? Well the first thing is, contrary to popular belief, you cannot gain an outer initiation by yourself however much you may want to. That concept was born out of the 'feel good' era where everyone was included and it was politically un-cool to exclude anyone. Telling people they can do what they want sells books and makes money, being truthful doesn't.

However, that does not mean that lone practitioners will never have initiation or will not be initiates. On an outer level, they will not have an initiation conferred upon them and they will not be part of a lodge/group, but if they are following their working magical path properly, they will obtain an inner initiation. It will not have a badge, certificate and a specific colored robe to go with it, but the practitioner will carry the inner marks of a magical line. The inner initiation links you to lines that acknowledge your wish to serve. The joy of this way is that there is nothing to show off and brag about, encouraging the initiate to concentrate on their work and not their egos.

A few years ago, I was talking to a friend, who is a very learned and magical person, and he was telling me about his progress in the ranks of the Golden Dawn. Although I would have considered him an adept when he first joined the lodge, he had to start at the beginning and work his way up. I think he was expecting to learn great things and have greater skills by the time he was conferred as an adept: he knew that in magic, there are always greater mountains to climb.

The day came, he was conferred with the title adept and was overjoyed. Three years later when we met up again, he told me how disappointed and let down he felt. He had finally seen that it was all about the status and title and not about the magic and knowledge. He had more in his little finger than the rest of them put together. He left the lodge and never looked back.

So what happens with a lone practitioner? Well the first thing to know is that if you do the work, are disciplined, focused and committed, you will make headway in the world of magic. When you begin to blossom you will find that you are gaining access to inner knowledge without realizing it, or without doing it consciously (accessing the great inner library), and you will also realize that you see people differently. I do not mean that in a conscious judgemental way, I mean it in a literal way. You will slowly see that some people look darker or murkier than others; some people look dead inside while others are bright and alive. You will notice some people look familiar and when you go to a conference/gathering/group of magical people you will recognize certain people as they will you. What has happened is that you have been conferred with an inner initiation into a magical stream of consciousness and others who are connected to that line become aware of you and you of them.

There is no great light that switches on, no day that can be marked as the day you were initiated; the awareness is gradual but profound. And the other interesting factor of an inner initiation is that you will be able to 'see' the false initiations. There are many people who, after paying hundreds if not thousands on courses leading to initiation, actually have nothing from an inner sense, and have merely been given an empty title. It has become so common that very few initiations these days are real. People will introduce themselves as an initiate and yet you 'know' that they are not: they do not hold the inner line that identifies them as such. Another interesting thing is that you will recognize someone with the inner markings and yet they have no direct link to magic that you are aware of. Often these are people who have carried it from another life and it has not yet awoken within them.

So as you can see, there are many natural or unintentional ways to have initiation as a lone magician. But are there any intentional ways that one can seek initiation as a lone seeker? Yes, of course there is.

Seeking Inner Initiation

For some, the knowledge that the mantle of Initiate has been draped across their shoulders is important, and often for very good reasons. Sometimes we do not trust our inner instinct, or we need more control over the situation than unintentional initiation will give. There is nothing wrong with that and in magic it is important to recognize the various facets of the personality and go with them rather than fight them. It is not a matter of letting go of inner striving; it is more a matter of allowing oneself to be normal and giving oneself boundaries that enhance the inner magic as opposed to suppressing. For myself, I am a natural control freak, so it is important magically for me to learn how to trust and let inner contacts do their share of the work. For someone who is more laid back and willing to let others do the work, it is important that they take responsibility for their development. So as you can see, it is not about hard fast rules, it is about approaching magical issues in a way that challenges you to expand and strengthen yourself.

The first step to seeking inner initiation is to ensure that this is a path that you truly want to walk. You are signing up for a length of service and training, and you will need to have reached a certain level of magical skill for it to work. So if you have decided after a week of reading magical books that you want to buy a black cloak and be an initiate, you can want all you like but it is not going to happen. If you have been reading, practicing and learning, and have come to a point where you are ready for deeper commitments, then it is probably time to go ahead with the initiation. Because you are choosing the time and place, and bring the focus of power to one point, it will be hard work but will have the same effect long term as a naturally conferred inner initiation.

The preparation

The physical preparation in truth not only cleans you up and gives you a blank slate, but it also magically begins to disentangle you from the outer world and takes you to the threshold of the inner. The first stage is setting the date so that you can prepare. For me personally, I would go by instinct and available date, and then check the astrological patterns rather than the other way around. This allows for alignments that you did not know about, and also other power dynamics that cannot be controlled.

The preparation begins the morning of the initiation. The timing should be to finish at midnight or close to, to use the depth of the stillness and also because the initiate always begins in death, night and the Underworld. The first thing in the morning should be about cleaning and sorting your living and magical space. Old, worn and useless things should be thrown away and not stored; the area where you sleep and do magic should be scrubbed down, organized and then magically cleaned (see Appendix 2: ritual cleansing). The reason for all the scrubbing and cleaning is that there must be no opportunity for inner parasites to attach to or interfere with the initiation and the two most prominent hang out places for parasites in a household is the bedroom and the magical space (magic and sex are both forms of energetic exchange which attract parasites). Parasites love clutter, dirt, and blocked areas: just as outer parasites like fleas, ticks etc love dirty, old, cluttered warm and damp spaces, so inner parasites like emotional clutter, dirty and blocked living areas, emotional baggage and areas of imbalanced energies. Inner and outer parasites tend to hang together, one feeds off your lifeblood and the other off your life energy. The outer cleaning triggers the inner, and the dumping of unused old belongings allows someone to let go old past times.

Once the living and magical area is clean, then clean the bathroom: it is the place where your body seeks cleansing, so itself should be clean. The same goes for trash, empty all bins, vacuum floors and put things away where they belong. Change half used candles for unused ones and place a bowl of consecrated salt and water in the magical space (see appendix 1: consecration of salt and water) where the initiation will take place. Leave the salt and water in the space to absorb any unhealthy residue, and only take it out a few minutes before the initiation begins.

Once the house is clean, and you have ensured that there is clean clothing to wear for the initiation, then it is time to eat and rest. Eat a [vegetarian] meal (to have no other resonance in your body but your own, so the inner contacts are sure they are working on just you and not the spirit of the cow whose butt cheek you have just eaten.) and then go rest/sleep. It is important to have this preparation sleep as the initiation actually started the minute you cleaned. The sleep begins the inner unraveling process in preparation for the power that is about to be downloaded into you.

Then comes the cleaning after you have slept. Set out clean clothing and go get a consecrated bath (Appendix 1). Once clean and dressed, it is time to prepare the space.

The Inner Initiation

Light fresh candles in each of the four directions and in the centre of the space. Be with the central flame, holding stillness within you and close your eyes. See the candle flames with your inner vision burning in each direction, and see through the flames to the inner contacts beyond the flames, waiting for you. When you have established that image in your head, open your eyes and walk to the east flame. Call out to the inner contacts in the direction of the east and ask them if they will acknowledge you as a student, a walker of the path, an initiate. Close your eyes and be still in the direction. See a being come forward through the flame and place a hand upon you. As they touch you, you will get a sense of what that line in the east demands. A particular demand or request may come into your head and you have to consider if you are willing to accept their conditions. It may be a request for a particular discipline, or task or they may ask you to give them something. If they want something and it is an object that belongs to you, then after the initiation you should dispose of it in a way that works for them (put in a river, bury it, burn it etc). Their requests may seem a little weird, but do not challenge it, either accept or refuse. If you refuse, they will probably withdraw their offer of initiation from that direction. It may be for the best if that line is making demands that you are unwilling to undertake.

Once you have finished with the contact in that direction, verbally thank them and voice your commitment to the magical line of that direction. Remember that anything you agree to or promise must be upheld. You repeat the action in the other three directions and the centre. You will come out with either five initiate lines, some of the five or just one – you will be connected into the streams of magical consciousness that is appropriate for you, and blocked from those that are not. Once you have been around all of the five directions, lie down in the magical space, and let your mind drift with the intention of finding the magical key that locks you into your initiation. If you fall asleep that is good. The magical key is a sigil that is unique to your combined initiatory lines, it is the sigil that other initiates will recognize you by and it is an inner mark that can be picked up by those with the inner sight. It may come to you straight away, or may slowly emerge in your mind over the coming days/weeks. Do not try to rush or pre-empt it: it is too easy for our minds to implant a sigil that we know or have seen. Often combined inner sigils are unique and yet familiar to many. Do not try and make it look like the magical sigils of grimoires etc, just let it be itself. You will know when it is the real one because you will see it everywhere, on walls, storefronts etc.

If possible, have a ring made that has the sigil stamped or engraved upon it. It you can do that, take it around the open directions to have it confirmed by the inner contacts. Leave it in dry salt the night before to strip any impurities out. If it is an old ring that you have chosen, then ritually strip it (appendix 2) before you engrave and take it to the contacts.

The inner initiation will slowly unfold or hit you like a wall; it all depends on how much power you were linked up to and what that is. Inner initiation that is conducted in this manner basically plugs you into the learning curves of specific inner lines of magic and prepares you for adeptship and subsequent consecration. The effects of inner initiation can be anything from feeling like a truck has hit you the day after, to feeling as though someone has just given you new batteries, or both. The days and weeks that follow are a settling in period before the real work kicks in. You will find, as the months unfold, learning is put in your path that is relevant to the tasks you promised to undertake/study. The power of the connection and its ability to sustain magical learning is wholly dependant on your willingness to continue working, studying and meditating. It is like being given a muscle implant - like all muscles, if you do not use them, they wither and die.

You may also find that some or all of the lines have specific codes of conduct that come with them. You will be made aware of them in no uncertain terms, and you will also be shown why. Such codes of conduct are never anything to do with morality; such a concept is for outer society and culture, not for spirituality and magic. The codes of conduct are there to shepherd you into a specific way of thinking, to strengthen your personality and strengthen your courage, while discouraging modes of behaviour that will ultimately weaken you. It also will demonstrate to you how the powers of Justice and Balance work in the magical world: it is all about energy and keeping the energy of fate patterns in a state of as near balance as possible.

If you diligently build the inner lines and learn from the code, then the inner contacts will uphold you through the next step of the initiate's work which is the training for adepthood and consecration.

The Adept and Consecration

Working towards true adeptship has nothing to do with courses, workshops, lodge grades, tests and stuffy modules. All of those things, no matter how well meaning (or just downright commercial) are of no real connection to true adeptship. Unfortunately, probably due to late 19th century Masonic influences in esoteric studies, the idea of adeptship has gone from understanding that a magician has reached a certain level of power -work, to a title given to people who have successfully passed exams, tests, and the like. It is a sad degeneration of a once powerful mantle that was bestowed upon those who worked in the true depths of magic: the mantle was given to those who displayed a deep understanding of the inner worlds, and an ability to magically work with power. These days, a couple of expensive weekend workshops spread over a year will give you the title adept, but it is indeed an empty title. True adeptship is earned in the inner worlds, not the magical workshop mall.

The consecration of the adept confers the inner powers of a specific lineage and connects them at a soul level to a long line of adepts before and after them. It is a link that cannot be broken either by death or magic: once a soul is consecrated, it stays consecrated. The consecration itself must be done physically through resonance and touch, and must be conducted by an adept who is capable of passing on a lineage.

Strengthening the Initiation

Once you have undergone the inner initiation, then it is important to strengthen the connections and begin training with a specific inner contact. In the days, weeks and months after the initiation, it is important to continue work in the directions the power of initiation flowed from, and to build upon it. That can be done by working in the ritual space on a regular basis, lighting the candles, working and learning with the magical implements, communing with the inner contact in that direction and designing and executing rituals that are relevant to the path ahead of you. If you have decided to work within a specific stream of magic for a length of time, you will need a contact to assist you in really learning about that. So for example if you are drawn to Egyptian magic, the first step is the study of that stream of power and to reach for a contact to guide you. Work with the contact first, and then read books or study history. Never do the books first: it is important that you get the reality of the magic first from the contact in its true form and then have confirmation by seeing it written. Popular magical forms have a vast array of books written, some useful and some not. It is very important to understand that these books are written by people who have no direct experience of the magical form, and are reconstructing things from ancient texts while adding their emotional and intellectual interpretations. There are authors who have had real and direct inner contact with such streams of magic and their writings are a mix of inner work and outer research. As an initiate of magic you need to be able to differentiate between the two and the only way to be able to do this is to have direct contact and experience via the contacts and practitioners of their own time and place.

Once you have had some direct contact and have worked a few times with contacts in the inner worlds and in their own times, it is time to look them up. After each inner working , write down everything you saw, heard and experienced, no matter how trivial it may seem. After a few months of working in that way, you should have enough material to compare with the written historical texts. The next step is to research/read history books, the ancient mythos, and look at the artwork, ritual engravings and tomb markings. Do not look to the magical books as most real historical information is not in those books, but in the stories and images of the ancient people. You will recognize certain things you had never noticed before, and you will begin to understand images and words that will pass most historians and theoretical magicians by. When you have exhausted the historical evidence, it is time to read the modern magical books on the subject. You will immediately be able to tell if the writer of the book has had real magical connection, or is simply writing opinion, theory and wishful thinking.

Getting a specific magical contact

If you are intent upon following a specific magical line, which is very important for building solid foundations in your work, then you will need a specific inner contact. There are a variety of ways to do this, and it might be an idea to try them all until one bears a positive result.

Like all magical work, some things work better than others depending on who, where and what point of the magical path you are on. Some people stay on the same path all their lives whereas others progress from one to another. All that truly matters is that you work hard and use your common sense.

The first step for gaining a specific inner contact is to decide to reach someone who was a priest/ess of their day or a true inner contact, i.e. they operate only from the inner realms and have no identifiable human life. Some inner contacts will dress as particular priest/ess magician from the space and time you are trying to reach. They are not trying to fool you; if you come across such a contact in deep magical work, chances are it is an inner being who possesses the knowledge you need and it is their way of telling you that they know about that subject. If you have reached out for a contact without proper boundaries, then it is possible to pick up a cross dressing parasite. So tread carefully and use your common sense.

If we stay with the theme of an Egyptian magical contact then an important early step will be to identify which part of the history of that land, which is a long and fruitful, is connected to the magic that you are interested in. The magic of the ancient world was always associated with or flowed from a deity. Once you have hit upon a deity that is close to where you wish to go in terms of power style, then reach out to a priest or priestess of that deity. Ensure from the very first step of this work that it is an initiate of a magical stream, and that you are looking to learn, not to serve. You will be asked at some point for your help in some matter; working with contacts is an exchange of skills, not a devotional relationship.

Set up your working space with the intention of reaching a teacher connected to the culture and deity of the magical stream you wish to learn from. As you light the central flame, affirm that request verbally and also from an inner point of view: let your inner voice be heard through the flame. Repeat the same request in each direction as you light the flames and once all flames are lit, stand in the centre with the central flame before you. Look into the central flame, focus in thought upon the image and name of the deity or known priest/ess of the magical stream that you wish to contact. Once you have a sense that you are fully focused, walk around the directions, pausing in front of each altar. Keep focussed on the person you wish to reach as you stand before each flame. When you have been around the directions a few times, you will be repelled by all but one direction, which seems to draw you in.

When that direction is established, walk around and blow out all other directions leaving the centre and the working direction lit. Stand before the directional flame and close your eyes. Using your voice, call out for a teacher from that magical line that would be willing to take you on as a student, to guide, teach and be with you. Using your inner vision, peer through the flame into the threshold of the world beyond. See yourself before the flame and the dividing line between the worlds as it runs through the flame. Beyond the flame is darkness and shadows. From the shadows, emerges a shape that takes on human form. That is your contact. The first contact may be shadowy and brief as your imagination struggles to work with the power. Tell the contact aloud what you want, the skills you wish to learn, the magical path you want to walk. The contact may tell you what they want in return and the deal is struck. Build an image in your mind of what they look like. It might have nothing to do with how they actually look; the point is that both you and the contact have a point of reference, a window to communicate through (a magical image).

Over the weeks and months, build up that magical image and work routinely on a daily or weekly basis with the contact in ritual and in vision. As the door is opened wider through regular contact, more information will stream through. Some of it will be clear and some not so. Some will come in dreams, some in working visions and some will come into your head as you work ritually. It is an amazing feeling when an ancient priest tells you an obscure fact about their magic and you look it up. It has happened many times to me and sometimes, what they say makes no sense whatsoever. I can look it up but it will appear nowhere. But a couple of years down the line the archaeological discovery will be made. Sometimes it never appears in a media/text book sense, but the information you are given sheds a whole new light upon the images, texts, and mythos of that time. The information or skills passed on to you are not to prove others wrong, they are to work with and learn from.

4
Developing Tarot Skills

Tarot is an important tool in the skills bag of a budding initiate, it is versatile and has many applications. It is used for divination, but can also be a great teacher of the stages of inner development and patterns of the magical world. The one thing to remember above all things in divination is that the success depends upon the relationship between you and the beings that use the cards as windows.

Some card decks are mere vocabularies, some are icons of deities and powers, and some are extensions of your own magical ability. The trick is knowing which deck is what. Every form has its limitations. There is also a limitation on sight: most sighted people see through a keyhole; they see a segment of the truth or the future, not the whole picture. That is why prophecies can seem so terrible and Armageddon like. If you look at say, the current situation in Iraq, and you look at it through a keyhole i.e. you see is a small section but to you it is the whole picture, it looks like the end of the world. So when you 'see' potential future events in the cards, keep in mind that you are seeing a small fragment.

The best way to approach Tarot, is to just get on and do. These days many magical training lodges have long drawn out courses in Tarot that go into minute detail into each card, creating a vision per card, a chapter per card, a weekend course per card. Why? Because it makes income, not because you need to know all that bullshit.

This chapter is about learning how to just get on and do, to get you walking down a path where Tarot will reveal itself as you go. You never stop learning with card divination, every time you think you have cracked it, another layer appears and off you go again. You are learning about the universe. I have been using cards since I was twelve years old, a wee while and I am still learning.

A reading

The best way to learn about Tarot is to do readings, many readings, about anything and everything. It is an extension tool of your mind and as such, practice is the way to perfect a skill. To get a good foundation in Tarot, choose a simple straightforward version of the Rider-Waite deck. It is the most commonly used deck and will give you a good understanding of the basic structure of Tarot. With a basic version of the deck and a straightforward book on the meanings of the minor and major arcana, you are ready to begin the long and fascinating journey. Don't fall into the trap of trying to make it a deep and mystical part of your training; if you do you will miss most of the truly magical aspects to this work. Divination is a natural part of humanity and the more you try to mystify it, the more you will become mystified and confused. Treat Tarot as an everyday part of your existence, and the more comfortable you will become. The keys of the mysteries are hidden among the images of the Rider Waite deck, but not in a way that you can crack them like a code. Just let them surface naturally over the years, their meanings changing as you change.

The next most important thing is the layout. Little thought is given to layouts; the layout is part of the deck, it puts the cards in context and without it the deck becomes inaccessible. Two things that set a reader up to fail are a badly designed deck and layout. Some decks and layouts are created as works of art, or philosophical musings, or experiments in magical dogmas. None of those decks will work to

```
                    ┌─────┐
                    │  1  │
                    │     │
                    └─────┘
  ┌─────┐                           ┌─────┐
  │  3  │                           │  2  │
  │     │                           │     │
  └─────┘                           └─────┘

  ┌─────┐                           ┌─────┐
  │  5  │                           │  4  │
  │     │                           │     │
  └─────┘       ┌─────┐             └─────┘
               │  6  │
  ┌─────┐       │     │             ┌─────┐
  │  8  │       └─────┘             │  7  │
  │     │       ┌─────┐             │     │
  └─────┘       │  9  │             └─────┘
               │     │
               └─────┘
               ┌─────┐
               │ 10  │
               │     │
               └─────┘
```

the degree that a properly focused deck would. So choose well. Layouts need to be relevant to the deck, and to the areas of magic you are working. The more generalized the layout, the more generalized the answers and insights. I work with a variety of layouts and choose one according to what I actually need to know. I use different layouts for questions regarding health, exorcism, ritual, and more general layouts for other questions.

Layouts

Let's look at a selection of general layouts that can be used for a wide variety of questions while also helping to imprint patterns of the mysteries. Both of the following have their roots in the greater mysteries.

The Tree of Life layout

The Tree of Life layout is one that is used in a teaching capacity in many of the better occult schools and lodges in the Western World. Not only is it fairly straightforward to gain information, it also instills the inner pattern of the Kabbalistic map of our world, which is what the Tree of Life is. By using it in a regular divinatory way, the subconscious absorbs little clues and snippets of information that surface regarding the mystery of the Tree.

There are many deep and meaningful insights into the Tree of Life layout, but if you get yourself tangled in them too soon and in the wrong way, you will not be able to get decent readings. The following interpretations of the layout are simple and straightforward. Their deeper meanings will surface to you when you need them.

The first three positions on the Tree of Life basically set out the story in relation to your question. Position four is the positive element of the story, five tells you what is withheld and six is the fulcrum or centre of the situation. Seven the emotions, eight the mind or magic, nine the family/bloodline/clan, and ten is your outcome.

So let's look at a reading

Question: a person is trying to choose which of two houses to buy. One looks better than the other, but the buyer has a weird feeling from that house. The buyer is a magician working magically in the home, so it is important to take that factor into considerations. The question is, show me what it would be like living in the better looking house?

```
                          10
                         earth
          4 earth                        moon

          3 cups                         tower

                        hanged
                        -man

          10                             queen
          fire                           swords

                       magician

                        Star
```

Overall the reading states that the house would be a working but, not a resting place, would be very hard to live in but would teach one a lot. So let's break it down. The first three, the story is about something that is a lot of money and is also about a sense of security

(10 earth), that is to do with stability (4 earth) but is also an unknown quantity or has hidden things (Moon).

The three central cards tell us that it needs work and will be a place of service, not socializing (three of cups withheld). The service (Hanged Man) alongside The Tower tells me that the property needs a lot of magical work/service to be done there, both for the land, the building and the community.

The ten of fire tells me there is a lot of magical power and that it needs focus and discipline to be able to enjoy living there (queen swords in emotions), but that it is the perfect place for a magician (magician in the position of the home/tribe) and The Star as the outcome tells us it is the start of a whole new path of learning. So as a reading I would interpret this reading as saying it would be a good and powerful working space, but would need a lot of attuning and it will never be a relaxing place to live.

How the question is asked is very important. Asking 'what would it be like living in the better looking house?' gives you many answers. It shows what it would be like to do magic there and what sort of house it would be like as far as relaxation and regeneration in concerned. If the question had been, 'is that the best house for me to buy?' The answer could have been in relation to financial investment, quality of the building, or family life, or general happiness etc, the options are endless and are not straightforward.

If the reader is really stupid, they would have asked, 'which is the best house to buy?' There are no cards that identify one house from another in this situation. It also leaves a lot of scope open in respect of opinion…the cards? You? The postman? And best house in what respect? So you can begin to see how the question is really important

```
                    ┌─────┐
                    │  3  │
                    └─────┘

  ┌─────┐           ┌─────┐           ┌─────┐
  │  6  │           │  7  │           │  8  │
  └─────┘           └─────┘           └─────┘

                    ┌─────┐
  ┌─────┐           │  2  │           ┌─────┐
  │  5  │       ┌───┴─────┴───┐       │ 12  │
  └─────┘       │      1      │       └─────┘
                └───┬─────┬───┘
      ┌─────┐       └─────┘       ┌─────┐
      │ 11  │                     │  9  │
      └─────┘                     └─────┘

                    ┌─────┐
                    │ 10  │
                    └─────┘

                    ┌─────┐
                    │  4  │
                    └─────┘
```

and has to be precise and to the point. Remember you are asking a set of cards that has a limited vocabulary.

The Desert Layout

Another layout which is also based upon magical patterns but gives overall information with a bit more detail than the Tree of Life I call the Desert. It is based around the inner landscape of humanity and is another octave of the Tree of Life. The Desert is a magical landscape that will become a major structure in the long term work of the initiate and eventually adept. Working with it in readings slowly builds the inner pattern within the psyche of those who work with it.

This layout gives you specific information regarding the location, timing and influences upon a situation whereas the Tree of Life layout gives energy dynamics. Let's break it down into sections.

Positions

1   The Body: Shows the body/property/centre of the subject in question

2   is Union; it sits across one and shows the subject matter's relationship.

3   The Stars; represents power moving into the realm of the subject, i.e. potential coming from the inner worlds and getting ready to manifest.

4   The Underworld; shows power moving into the past and the deep storage of the Underworld.

5   The Door; shows what is completely past.

6   The Wheel; shows the current/path/influences/trend the subject is going through.

7   The Mountain; shows the difficulties that have to be overcome.

8   The Temple; is the position of temple/magic/active inner realm.

9   The Hearth; is the home/family.

10   The Cave: represents people or situations that are falling into the past.

11   The Dreamer: is sleep/dreams and shows what is happening in the sleep world of the subject. It can also represent what is happening in a visionary sense, if they are active visionary magicians.

12   The Gates; is the future manifestation of the power that was shown in position three. The cards that fall in 3 and 12 can often be read together, as can 2 and 5. Note: all of these positions have names and images that are a part of the inner desert and can be read in context to such inner realms. They can also be represented on cards so that the card and position can be read together; that is a very accurate form of reading cards.

So let's have a look at the layout at work. Asking the same question as before, lets see what the desert layout had to say.

Position 1&2 ace earth/pentacles crossed by The Devil.
3 is the 10 fire
4 is The Fool
5 is The Knight of water/cups
6 in the Wheel of Fortune
7 is the 9 of fire
8 is the Priestess
9 is 5 of swords

10 is 9 of swords

11 is 8 of swords

12 is The Hanged Man

Position 1 tells us that the body of the subject matter is earth (bricks and mortar) and what crosses it is a relationship with a powerful consciousness or entity. What is being formed in the future of this place is power (10 fire) and what has fallen into the Underworld and therefore the past is foolish emptiness. Combine this with the knight of cups in the fifth position and you have an idea what the previous owner was a man who was too emotional and unstable to be able to operate the powers in that land/house properly. This gives you insight into how power lines up for the magician; because there is a possible future with the magician in that house, power is already starting to line up in the inner worlds ready for the decision.

In the position of current trends is The Wheel, showing that the partnership of house and magician would change old patterns. What would have to be overcome is the level of power (9 fire) and its potential danger, the lesson of this position is to tread wisely and learn a major lesson about handling power. This position, which I call the mountain, will push you to your outer limits but never gives you more than you can cope with.

In the position of the temple is The Priestess, which means that this property has active inner lines and there is a contact, which is female. In position 9, which is the home and tribe, the 5 of swords tell us that the home will not be a peaceful place. 5 of swords brings arguments and irritations, not major disruptions, but enough to know that you will not get much down time in that house.

The Cave, position 10, is 9 of swords and shows that difficulties with negative or dark power are slowly fading into the past. This means that working within such a difficult house will most likely strengthen you to the point whereby such negative power will not affect you too greatly in the future. I have personally found that the nine of swords and nine of fire/wands often appear in a reading together and when they do, they signify that negative powers flowing to you are not natural - they are sent by magic, ill wishing or deception. In this reading, I would say that the person asking the question is on the receiving end of some unhealthy or negative magic and this house will help the person to learn how to handle power and how to become strong enough to deal with such nasty actions.

11, the position of the dreamer shows the 8 of swords, which in that position tells me the person is going to have almost continuous nightmares and there will be a lot of magical activity in the house. In such circumstances the worst thing would be to take sleeping pills. When such activity shows in the dreams, the person sleeping will actually be working hard fighting unhealthy energies, which will be part of the service for that property. If the person takes sleeping pills, it will render them helpless in the face of such power and will damage them. That will be why the previous tenant was emotionally unstable. In such situations, despite the bad nights, the tenant will probably have enough sleep to keep functioning. I have lived like that for five years and used to go to a motel every so often just to sleep peacefully.

Position 12, The Gates, show The Hanged Man, - service. It shows that living in that house will be training for powerful service in the future.

So to sum the reading up, I would tell the person that if they chose that house, it would be bloody hard work: they would learn a lot, get no peace, but would come out the other end fighting fit and able to take on anything the world throws at them.

Readings are a mix of the cards, positions and common sense... they will not do all the work for you, as a reader you have to allow your own insight to kick in and fill the gaps rather than platitudes and wishful thinking.

Tarot Taboos

There are a variety of Tarot taboos, some of which are useful and some of which are just plain silly. Often the taboos are stated in Tarot books without explanation. This makes it difficult to differentiate between what should be noted or ignored; in the end personal experience and common sense are the only way forward. Let's have a look at the most common taboos.

A reader cannot read for themselves

This is just not true. It is difficult to step back and be impartial when reading for yourself. Most of the time when readers read Tarot for themselves, they are looking at low level questions of; will I get a lover/money/job. Such questions are not only a waste of time for an initiate but also take the attention away from necessary work and down the blind alley of trying to control one's universe. If a reader does not like or believe what the cards foretell, then they will read again and again until it becomes more palatable. It is an easy road to get stuck down but if you use your common sense, you can read pretty well for yourself . . .the key is to be detached. And that is a larger aspect of magical training in general; to be able to put wants and needs to one side, and to be able to look at a situation from a non emotional stand point. We have to be able to look outside of or, beyond ourselves, that way we can use the information we are given in a calm dispassionate way that will ensure its balanced and productive use.

The cards need to be wrapped in a certain colored silk

To which my reply is… 'oh whatever'… No they do not… for years I kept my cards wrapped in a plastic bag and had them shoved at the bottom of my bottomless purse that also had a spanner, screwdriver, wooden nickels, pepper spray, raisins and various other bits and bats that were totally unconnected but often came in useful. It is helpful but not essential to have a piece of cloth that you can lay the cards on when you do a reading. On an outer level this protected the cards from whatever was on the table surface (or floor… I often read on the floor) and also stops the energetic gloop that can accompany some readings from seeping onto the working surface.

You cannot read after dark

Really? Cough….

The cards must only be shuffled by the person asking the question.

Who shuffles the cards is completely up to the style and wishes of the reader. Personally I shuffle the cards for whoever wants a reading; I don't like other people handling the cards and leaving their residue upon them; it interferes with my ability to have a clear working communion. But that's just me. You have to work out for yourself which works best for you. When as a young girl I first started reading, I noticed that when people shuffled the cards, they get a build up of sticky inner goo that made me feel uncomfortable. So by about the age of eighteen, I stopped letting people touch my cards at all. But then I know very successful readers who never shuffle the cards themselves.

The person you are reading about or for needs to be there with you

Wrong… only you put limits on what and who you can read for. The key to reading about anyone and anything is to focus your mind very clearly on what you want to know or who you are reading about, and then do your reading. Some readers can only read for someone if they are in front of them as they need to be able to 'read' their energies etc. But that is a personal and individual thing, not a restriction. There are no limits on who, what, and when you can read for; the only limit is the imagination of the reader.

It is an extremely important fact to understand that magic, cards etc are only restricted by what you put in the way of yourself…

Keeping yourself and the deck clean

One thing that does happen in readings, no matter whom or what the readings are about is that the cards will accumulate a kind of inner dirt or residue. This manifests itself as the cards feeling grimy and sticky. It is important to gain sensitivity towards inner residue and dirt as it could prevent a whole lot of magical health problems in the future. The best way to get the feeling of inner dirt is to wash your hands with soap and a handful of salt, and then go to a thrift or junk store and handle old things like rings, statues etc. Your hands will feel sticky or grimy. Another way to do it is to salt clean your hands and then handle your own Tarot deck if you have used it a lot. Notice how it feels and how it makes your hands feel. Clean the deck and then feel them again, they will feel completely different. Smudging can help to maintain a deck after each reading but it does not clean as thoroughly as salt. Using smoke to maintain the deck after each reading will ensure that they do not need salting quite as much. A lot of people use sage because it is what Native Americans use, but that is not a part of my culture nor my practice. It is always better to try and use something that is relevant to the magical path upon which you walk. I use Frankincense mixed with a tree resin that comes from an evergreen in the Romanian mountains (exotic huh…)

Cleaning a deck

Keeping a deck clean is simple but necessary and should be done regularly if you use it a lot. You will need a plastic Tupperware type long container and a large bag of salt. To clean the deck, just put it in the container and pour the salt over the cards until they are covered. Move them around so that the salt gets in between and when you are sure that they are well covered, put the container with the cards in a safe place overnight. The following morning, take them out of the salt and give them a good shake to get the salt residue off. Spread them out on a cloth to air for an hour and they should be ready for use again.

To smudge them, have some frankincense or similar resin burning on charcoal and hold the cards over them, moving them around to ensure all are touched by the smoke. Then 'wash' your hands in the smoke. If you use a cloth to wrap the cards, then ensure that you wash it regularly and that some salt is in the water. There is no ceremony to cleaning cards; it is just regular maintenance. Some books will tell you that there are complex ritual ways to clear cards with invocations etc. Just remember that drama sells books more than reality and common sense.

Cleaning yourself

The first rule for keeping yourself clean after a reading is to wash your hands with salt and soap as soon as you have finished. Do not do or touch anything else until you have cleaned your hands. If the reading session was particularly hard or the subject matter was very unhealthy, then also rub some salt over your 'third eye' area and wash your face. If you were doing a series of readings on powerful magical subject matter like demonic issues, or difficult readings like around a suicide, not only should you clean your hands and forehead, you will need to clean your whole body. Take a consecrated salt bath to clear off any residue, any connections to beings that may have latched on to you etc. The instructions for a salt bath are listed in Appendix 1.

Tasks for getting good at Tarot

Developing skills in Tarot is like any other form of art; it's all about practice. The first step of developing a good practice routine is to keep a log of readings. Every time you do a reading, copy down the layout and cards and your interpretation. Date it and don't forget to write down the questions. Do this as a major discipline for at least five years and keep the log books tucked away safely. Whatever it was that you read for, write down the actual physical outcome underneath the reading so that you can look to see how accurate or not you were. If you were off base, then look at the reading again, look at the positions of the cards and at what actually happened. The cards will show you how they were interpreting the event and you will be able to see where you went wrong. One great lesson you will learn from this above all other lessons is that the cards are always right; it is your skill as an interpreter that wasn't. You will learn far more from your mistakes than you will from studying any book. Keeping a reading diary is a major tool in that learning.

Once you have your diary in place you need to do readings that you can look back on. Doing many readings on a wide variety of subjects is a great way to learn. So for example, if there is an election coming up, do readings on each candidate, look at their next 12 months, look at their health, their family life, ask if they will or won't be elected. Record all of the readings in your diary and a year later look back at the answers and how you interpreted them. Do year readings for celebrities, for public figures etc so that you can track outcomes through the media. What you may find is that although you asked to see the next 12 months, you may be shown the next major happening in their life, which may be further away than 12 months. Just bear that in mind and if it has not happened after 12 months, keep watching.

I was working with a Tarot group in Cambridge Massachusetts in the 90s looking at political figures of the time. As it was coming up to election time we looked at Bill Clinton, to see if he was going to get in. We also did a 12 month reading. The reading showed a hidden daughter figure that would cause a scandal. Obviously now we know it was not a hidden daughter, but the public knowledge of the affair took longer to come to light, so at the end of the 12 months, we saw nothing that related to the reading. It came out a wee bit later. Sometimes it comes out years later; hence it is important to keep all the diaries. It is also a good idea to use readings to track your magical development and do readings on a 12 monthly basis to monitor your magical training.

Read about anything to stretch your and the deck's ability to push beyond boundaries. Look into death, ask questions that would not normally occur to you. Think carefully about how you phrase your question so that you get a clear answer. Ask about the health of a bodily organ in someone; ask about the future history of a car, anything that you can then verify in the future. The more readings you do on a wide variety of subjects, the better a reader you will become. There are no limits. Just understand that your ability to interpret the readings will probably be off and that the skill of interpretation will possibly take years to perfect. So don't freak out or someone else out over a reading's conclusions, because there will be a big chance, particularly in the first couple of years, that you may be incorrect.

Magical dynamics of Tarot, both good and bad

When you read Tarot beyond just the silly every day 'am I going to get rich', there are a variety of energetic/power dynamics that come into the play that you need to be aware of.

Cards as doorways

The first and most important point that you always have to keep at the back of your mind is that when you do a reading for a being or a realm, laying out the cards opens a conduit to that being or place. This only happens if you have been working and training in visionary magic: once you open the door to the inner worlds, it never really shuts. So when you 'read' about a place or being, the door that was propped slightly open becomes opened wide and any beings involved in that realm can come through if they are allowed to.

In magic, intent and focus of thought is everything (which should be a mantra and also written in large letters upon your forehead). That focus and intent can be used to create boundaries that will enclose a reading and make it safe. If you are reading about an issue that involves other worlds or beings, light a candle and focus it on the void or upon the magical pattern of the magical working space. Even if you are no-where near your magical working/patterned room, lighting the candle with the focus of that room will superimpose it over the place where you are doing the reading. You tune the two places together so that you are working in a magical space with boundaries.

If you are communing with a being through the reading, or looking for answers relating to the being, working within the boundaries will make it safer. You can ask the being direct questions using the Tarot, but when you have finished, ensure that you mix the deck up to break up the reading, and that the deck is immediately put in salt to break any hold it may have upon the deck. They can use decks as windows into our world, which is often not a good thing. Wash yourself properly with salt after such a reading.

Narrowing fate

The other dynamic that can become a problem for a magician using Tarot, is the narrowing of fate. When you read for a situation the first time, a variety of options of future outcomes may present themselves. The more a reading is focused on a specific event and read over and over for, the more the fate options are closed down and the final future outcome is set. This can be very dangerous as it can take away the chance for inner powers to flow through a fate situation to assist in a magical path. The advice is: only repeat a reading or try a reading on the same question from a different angle if you did not understand the original outcome the first time around. Do not keep asking the same question: you run the possibility of damaging future options.

Another, more important dynamic with the narrowing of fate with readings is interrupted fate. If you have pissed off a very skilled magician (which is something I did a lot in my younger days) they may launch a magical attack upon you that changes your fate. If you are under such an attack, it is important to keep an eye on your fate path by way of readings. If it is interfered with, you can work out through readings how to restore the fate to how it looked before the attack, or as close in as you can get to restoring it.

Responsibility

This is something that is very important in the field of divination in general: whenever you peer into the future (or past, Tarot works both ways) you carry a great deal of responsibility, not only in light of the magical dynamics previously discussed, but way of privacy and compassion. If you are doing a basic reading for someone, do it with him or her alone and with no one else in the room. What transpires in that room is private and should always remain so. Never read couples together: that was a mistake I made when I was young. Often people are dishonest to each other and it will show in a reading. So diplomacy can be very important, as can tact and compassion.

Someone who was learning the skill of Tarot once offered me a reading, he wanted to practice. He was what I would call an archetypical *Aspergers* type with no social skills but very good sight. He told me that in my late 40s I would be terribly ill and could die in my 50s, but that there was a chance I would survive. I was already aware of this situation, but the way he put it so bluntly, with such cold lack of emotion caused me to give him a very harsh telling off. If he had come out with something like that to a person off the street he could have driven them to suicide or at least deep depression.

I was cursed very seriously a few years back (by a disgruntled ex husband) and it altered my life path considerably. My body was badly impacted by the strength of the attack (the energy of many students was used), and along with usual life stresses and an inherited autoimmune disease, it has shortened the life span that I would have had. There is a possibility that I could die in my mid 50s, but then I could get knocked over tomorrow. I have no problem with that prediction and I trust my inner contacts to guide me through this period of my life and as long as I complete the work I promised to do, it really is not such an issue. If I am meant to survive, I will. If not, it has been a wild life! The problem that I had with the reader is that he was unaware whether I was OK with this situation and it had not occurred to him that I might find it disturbing. That lack of awareness made him a loose cannon in magical terms and he should not be reading for other people (which I told him in no uncertain terms). All in all, Tarot both as a deep magical, and as a 'fortune telling' tool comes with a lot of responsibility attached and the basic overall advice is – use common sense and think very carefully about the impact that your words may have!

Summary

Walking the path of magic is something that will change you profoundly forever. There is knowledge to be found in the most curious places, and many teachers have fragments to pass on in one way or another. But to really condense advice down to a few paragraphs for those starting out in magic, or struggling alone in their training, well, that is a challenge! So here goes.....

Prejudgement: Don't assume that because someone dresses in fancy robes, has grand titles and loads of books published with New Age publishers that they are going to be useful or good teachers. Similarly, don't think because someone looks normal and does not have a fancy sounding name that they do not have something to teach you. Remember, the Goddess often appears as a bag lady on the street, and the grumpy old man in front of you on the train is really an angelic being! Magical learning can often come from the strangest of places.

Discernment: the greatest skill of all. Learn to read with discernment, chose your books wisely, read the words with the bullshit meter on full blast, and if what is written seems to be using a complex, confusing and archaic language, then chances are the writer has not got a clue.

Glamour: one of the biggest magical traps of all. When you learn how to work with contacts and power for the first time, the realization of what is possible becomes overwhelming and you can end up walking straight into the glamour trap. There are two sides to the glamour trap; being glamorized by someone, and then glamorizing yourself. Being glamorized by someone is where you are easily taken in or impressed by their abilities to the point where you begin to hero or guru worship them. This is very unhealthy and unnecessary; it is one thing to be impressed by someone, it is another to worship. Do not go down that route, it can have a very unhappy ending. Humans are humans, respect is great, pedestals are not.

But being glamorized by your own magical ability is a very dangerous trap to walk into and it is one that catches many potentially great magicians and destroys them (and I have married many of them). No matter what you discover, what you succeed in achieving, remember you are not the messiah, you are not a perfect master and you are not going to save the world. It is very common when people first experience power flow through them to get the idea that they are something special. You are not special; you have just learned the first step in a sacred art form, the knowledge of which was far more extensively realized by your ancestors. We have regressed magically over the last 5000 years and are slowly clawing our way back to the rudimentary understandings that were so common before we realized we knew it all.

A good example of this was a website I came across a couple of years ago. A young magician had been working in the inner realms and had crossed the Abyss. To him and the books he had read, he had just achieved mankind's the greatest step. Unfortunately for him, the books he had been reading were basically written by someone who was not that clued in. The crossing of the Abyss is a step within magical training that is considered normal and is a foundational movement that heralds the beginning of more serious work in the various realms of power and divinity. The poor hapless magician put up a website to celebrate the fact that he was now an adept of the highest order and offered to teach. There will come a day when he has a very red face (hopefully).

One other very important thing to remember that will really help you move forward on your magical path is self-responsibility. If you mess up, you are to blame, no one else. When things go badly in our lives, or we do stupid things, it is easy to turn around and blame everyone and everything around us for our failings and misfortunes. But by doing that, the process of learning through experience is short-circuited and we end up going nowhere. It can sometimes take a lot of soul searching to see how often we bring things down upon ourselves, or dodge responsibility. But that is something that cannot be done for very long on a powerful magical path; at some point you will be put in a situation where you face yourself. So to make life easier, it is much better to be true to yourself; accept the harsh reality of your part in the wrongdoing/disaster and move on.

I hope this book has been useful in some way or another and that you discover some of the wondrous and truly amazing things that lie in wait for those who step out onto the path of Magical Knowledge.

I do have a website www.theinnerlibrary.org for those who are interested, which has further material for people to work with.

Appendix 1
The consecration of
salt and water

This method is used to strip and tune salt and water for cleansing a body or space. The ritual wording can also be used to strip an object. If you are using this ritual to strip an object, you would only need recite section A over the object.

Use the first two fingers of blessing to point at the object and where you see + it means make the sign of an equal armed cross over whatever you are working on.

A - Recite over a bowl of salt while pointing first two fingers:

"I exorcise thee creature of the earth by the living gods+ the holy gods+ the omnipotent gods+ that thou mayest be purified of all evil influence in the name of Adonai, lord of all angels and men. (Use the flat of the hand over the salt) creature of the earth adore thy creator. In the name of God the father+ and God the mother+ I consecrate thee to the service of the gods and goddesses".

B - Recite over a bowl of water or a bath of water while pointing first two fingers:

"I exorcise thee creature of the water by the living gods+ the holy gods+ the omnipotent gods+ that thou mayest be purified of all evil influence in the name of

Elohim Savoth, lord of all angels and men. (flat of the hand) creature of the water adore thy creator. In the name of God the father+ and God the mother+ I consecrate thee to the service of the gods and goddesses."

Recitation of pouring: pouring the water and salt together; recite the following as you pour the salt into the water.

"Lord God father of the heavens above, great Goddess, mother of the earth below my feet, grant that this salt will make for health of the body and this water for health of the soul. (pour salt into the water)Grant that they may be banished from whence they are used, all powers of adversity, every artifice of evil shall be banished into the outer darkness in thy holy names, Amen."

Once the salt and water are poured together, the mix is ready to cleanse and purify anything it touches. For a ritual bath, consecrate the whole of the bath water, consecrate a dish of salt and then pour in the salt while doing the recitation of pouring. To cleanse a room, this preparation can be used with the recitation of exorcism listed below: sprinkle the consecrated salt water around the directions as you recite.

Appendix 2
Recitation of
the basic exorcism

This can be recited in a space, while sprinkling consecrated salt and water to cleanse a room, building or object. It can also be uttered over a ritual bath to strip the person of anything that is magically attached to them. It will work as a basic cleansing and exorcism for a person, place or thing when the infestation is a parasitical or low level beings. A true exorcism however requires a little more…

Using the first two fingers, trace a triangle in the air (or over a bath) marking the three points as you begin the recitation of the three names of G-D (Father, Mother and Holy Spirit). For the rest of the recitation, use the first two fingers and point to the centre of the triangle you have just traced in the air.

"In the name which is above every other name, and in the power of the Father, and of the Mother and of the Holy Spirit, I exorcise all influences and seeds of evil from this body/room/object. All chained or bound angels who are not in the service of God but of man and magic, I free them of their bindings and release them to the wilderness before God to be in God's service. I exorcise all demons, parasites, ghosts, thought-forms, golems, curses, spells and bindings from this body/room and spirit. I cast upon them the spell chains and I cast them into the outer darkness where they shall trouble not this servant of God Amen, Amen Selah."

Appendix 3
Making a Specific Talisman

A talisman can be used for a limited length of time when it is really needed. Such circumstances would normally be illness, a powerful magical attack when you cannot give it your full attention, or having to go into a place that you know is possessed by a being that is very dangerous. If you wear a talisman too much your body and spirit will not be strengthening against magical attacks or against dangerous beings: it will prevent your inner immune system from performing properly. But there are times when we need an extra bit of help, and those are the times to use a talisman.

First choose a ring or necklace that you would be willing to wear all the time for a while. It is best if it does not have magical or spiritual imagery as that would filter the contact. Something that is metal or stone would be best and would hold power for long enough to be affective. So for example a semi precious stone in a plain setting would be great. A real magical talisman is not a fancy magical seal or sigil festooned medal, it is what is put in it that matters, not what it looks like. Place it in a bowl of dry salt for 24 hours to magically strip it before you begin working.

Set up your work/sacred space with the four altars in the four directions and one in the centre. Have the talisman on the altar and light the central flame, while using the vision of the void. Once the inner flame is lit, go and light the candle in the east, then the south, west and north before returning to the central flame. Go around the directions, this time spending time in each and call the inner contacts that you have made, asking them to the threshold of the flame and if they would be willing to help you with your work.

Once all four directions have contacts ready, pick up the talisman and start in the east. Hold the talisman over the flame and beyond it, so that it has passed over the threshold. See the inner contact with your inner vision and ask them to put into the talisman whatever would be necessary to help and protect you magically during this difficult time. Put the talisman in your left hand and hold your right hand over the object. Using your inner vision, see the inner contact place their hand over yours and feel the power flowing through your hand and into the talisman. You will feel when it is finished, and when it has, step back and thank the inner contact for their help.

Repeat the same process in each direction, but just remember to be as unconditional as possible: ask for help to protect you magically. That is a very simple request. It will not protect you from mundane physical danger, but it will from both inner and outer danger that is instigated by magic. By being so simple, the talisman will cover all bases. If you start a shopping list of what you want protecting from, there is a very good chance you will not mention or even know about every risk that you are subject to.

Once the talisman has been touched by all four inner contacts, place it on the central altar and place your right hand over it. Ask God the Father of the stars above, and God the Mother of the Underworld below to bless and protect you through the talisman, allow that blessing to flow through your hand and into the talisman.

Leave the talisman on the central altar and go around the directions, thanking the contacts, closing the gates and putting out the candles, always working east, south, west and finally north. Leave the central flame burning with the talisman on the altar, and leave the room for a while so that it can 'cook': as the magical process has to be completed without human presence.

Once ready, go back in, take the inner flame into yourself and blow out the candle. Put the talisman on and do not take it off for anything. Not for a shower, not for a change of clothes, nothing. It must stay in contact with your body at all times to work. Once it is full of impact and is no longer working, a talisman will often break or shatter, or will not stay on you anymore. That is the time to either make a new one, or test the water to see if it is safe to come out.

Don't use talismans unless you really have to; it is a last resort. But only using them as an emergency stopgap, you will find you gain a great deal of magical strength over the years. Those who wear talismans all the time tend to eventually end up weak and damaged as their own inner immune systems have not been activated or challenged.

Index

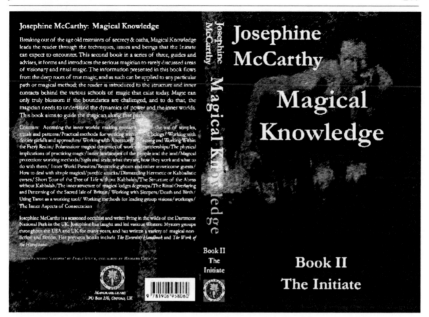

Magical Knowledge: Book II

The Initiate by Josephine McCarthy

ISBN: 9781906958060 £12.99 / $23 / 344pp / paperback

TraditionBreaking out of the age old restraints of secrecy & oaths, *Magical Knowledge* leads the reader through the techniques, issues and beings that the Initiate can expect to encounter. This second book in a series of three, guides and advises, informs and introduces the serious magician to rarely discussed areas of visionary and ritual magic. The information presented in this book flows from the deep roots of true magic, and as such can be applied to any particular path or magical method; the reader is introduced to the structure and inner contacts behind the various schools of magic that exist today. Magic can only truly blossom if the boundaries are challenged, and to do that, the magician needs to understand the dynamics of power and the inner worlds. This book aims to guide the magican along that path.

Contents: Accessing the inner worlds: making contacts without the use of temples, rituals and patterns/Practical methods for working with angelic beings/ Working with deities: pitfalls and approaches/ Working with Ancestors/ Accessing and Working Within the Faery Realm/ Polarization: magical dynamics of work and partnerships/ The physical implications of practicing magic/Inner landscapes of the people and the land/Magical protection: working methods/Sigils and seals: what they are, how they work and what to do with them/ Inner World Parasites/Removing ghosts and other unwelcome guests/ How to deal with simple magical/psychic attacks/Dismantling Hermetic or Kabbalistic curses/ Short Tour of the Tree of Life without Kabbalah/The Structure of the Abyss without Kabbalah/The inner structure of magical lodges & groups/The Ritual Overlaying and Patterning of the Sacred Isle of Britain/ Working with Sleepers/Death and Birth/Using Tarot as a working tool/ Working methods for leading group visions/workings/The Inner Aspects of Consecration

Order direct from
Mandrake of Oxford, PO Box 250, Oxford, OX1 1AP (UK)
Phone: 01865 243671 (for credit card sales)
Prices include economy postage
online at - www.mandrake.uk.net,
Email: mandrake@mandrake.uk.net

Lightning Source UK Ltd.
Milton Keynes UK
UKOW041527130712

195938UK00001B/221/P